RENEWED VISION

Missions Programming
in the
Local Church

RENEWED VISION

Missions Programming
in the
Local Church

Esther F. Wilson

REGULAR BAPTIST PRESS
1300 N. Meacham Road
P.O. Box 95500
Schaumburg, Illinois 60195

Library of Congress Cataloging in Publication Data

Wilson, Esther F., 1934—
   Renewed vision.

   1. Missions—Study and teaching—
Handbooks, manuals, etc. I. Title.
BV2090.W55   1985   254'.6   85-8246
ISBN 0-87227-103-X

RENEWED VISION: MISSIONS PROGRAMMING IN THE
LOCAL CHURCH
© 1985
Regular Baptist Press
Schaumburg, Illinois
Printed in U.S.A.
All rights reserved

Contents

Introduction

I will instruct thee and teach thee in the way which thou shalt go: I will guide thee with mine eye (Ps. 32:8).

Why another book on missions? After all, there is only so much that can be written on this subject. Missions has been widely covered by our Bible scholars, pastors and their wives, along with many of our fine missionaries.

Why another book on missions? The message is still **not** getting beneath the surface of the skin, into the blood stream, and beating in the pulse of believers throughout the world.

Why another book on missions? The Lord has definitely impressed me—housewife, mother and grandmother—to share the practical side of missions with all who are interested.

To preface this book of ideas, successes and failures in missions, I would retrace my steps to the first awakening to missions in my own life.

It began back in 1944 when the Lord used a faithful Sunday School teacher to plant and cultivate the seed which would blossom forth some eighteen years later into a full-blown ministry in missions. Yes, it was the in-depth teaching of the life of Paul along with talks about the Baptist mission work in Burma that started me on my way.

In my adult life, the sensitivity of my pastor helped to direct me into a field of service where he felt I could be used of the Lord. With some reservation and apprehension, I attended an area-wide ladies' meeting at my pastor's request. The guest speaker was Miss Gladys Baines, Director of the Women's Department of Baptist Mid-Missions. My heart is full-to-overflowing with appreciation for this dear saint of

God and for the way the Lord used her to set me on fire for missions.

A faithful Sunday School teacher, a concerned pastor, a dedicated missionary, and especially an understanding husband launched me into twenty years of missions.

So, **why another book on missions?** To answer the pastors, their wives and church laymen who have written, phoned, or visited to request some assistance in their missions programs. This book will cover topics which will benefit your Ladies' Missionary Fellowship and your church missions committee.

Only to be used of Thee, dear Lord.
— *Esther Wilson*

PART 1

Organization

1
Missions
and the young church

Missions should be part of the initial groundwork for the budding young church. The thrust needs to come from the **pastor** — *he* must have the **vision!** The work will only go as far as the pastor can see — "Where there is no vision, the people perish." The small church can become actively involved in missions and not draw from the efforts needed in establishing a new church.

"As newborn babes, desire the sincere milk of the word, that ye might grow thereby" — this should be your approach to missions. Start off *easy* and build *slowly,* but *steadily!* Why? People shy away from the unknown, and if it is shoved down their throats, they will balk! This is one good reason for pastoral teaching on the subject, before hitting the people with "do this, do that."

If you, as a church, start tithing every offering — even from the first time the hat is passed at the organizational meeting — the habit for developing a healthy missions program will have started. Take the money "right off the top" and place it in the missions account.

There are many avenues of missions to be explored by the young church and it should be one of the most exciting and involved areas of service. Aside from the pastor, you need at least one person ready to start developing a missions program. It is *very important* that this person and the pastor are on common ground and share the same objectives concerning missions.

The following are some ideas for a beginning that will not overload your people.

11

1. *Messages from the pulpit on missions* — given by the pastor or a visiting missionary. Have a missions Sunday once a month (morning and/or evening).

2. *Invite missionaries to speak* — allow time for questions and for fellowship. The missionary's family, if they can come, will create an interest among the children. They will remember the missionary's children who sat in their Sunday School class or played with them.

3. *A mini-conference* — the very first year! This is so important— it is the frosting on the cake. Get your people involved in every phase of the preconference preparations. A well-run conference will do more for your church than any of the other special meetings you may have during the year.

(Note: Missionaries invited to your church need to be of "like precious faith" — and *name. Baptist* churches should support *Baptist* missionaries! If you have even one questionable mission board represented, it exposes your people to unhealthy mission policies. This also creates havoc later when you try to undo the harm that was done.)

4. *Mission bulletin board* — a very effective tool. It should include a Scripture verse about missions, a map, prayer cards, prayer letters, personal notes and possibly missions articles or pictures. The materials used should be attractively displayed and up-dated.

5. *Mission prayer time* — every Prayer Meeting! Missionaries send prayer letters to be *read,* and requests for prayer are for *prayer!*

6. *Keep a file on all visiting missionaries* — and a separate file for each missionary under support. This file should include an information sheet, prayer card or other photograph, prayer letters, and personal correspondence. These records are valuable, especially for new members of the missions committee in the years ahead.

7. *A missions photo album* — ask the church "camera bug" to take pictures of visiting missionaries and set up an interesting record of special times at the church.

8. *Sunday School classes* — let the children and teens

prepare a missions corner in their classes with a missions map, prayer cards and curios. A missions lending library is an excellent way to stimulate missionary interest.

9. *Birthdays and anniversaries* — some folks just thrive on projects such as these. They enjoy sending cards and gifts to missionaries. Make the dates available and encourage faithful remembrance of the missionaries' special days.

10. *Christmas gifts!* This can be such a blessing to your church. Start early (for shipping purposes) and make it a fun project for your church family. Check with the missionaries on sizes, colors and special likes or dislikes.

There they are: ten simple ways to launch your church into missions, making it a blessing instead of a burden.

A healthy church will be supporting missionaries by the end of the first year. Much spiritual discernment is needed in deciding which missionaries to support. Young Christians will go for Mr. Personality and overlook a more dedicated missionary. Thus, it is advisable to use mature Christians on your missions committee. If there are no mature Christians in the church, then the pastor should be allowed the privilege of making the support recommendations.

As time passes and the church gets well situated spiritually and physically, ease into a more elaborate missions program. Much prayer and wisdom is needed in channeling your mission endeavors.

2
Missions and the teenage church

Having completed your first year in missions, *STOP* and evaluate your missions program! Have you succeeded in completing the initial ten steps of organizing a healthy missions program in your church? Are you prepared to enter phase two of this important building program?

It has been said many times, "You can give without loving; but you cannot love without giving."

Part of a little chorus picked up many years ago at a Bible conference says:

It's love, it's love,
it's love that makes the world go round
It's you, it's you,
it's you that makes the love go round . . .

Galatians 6:10 states very clearly the need for Christians to be concerned for others of the faith. Yet, many times we run across nearsighted Christians in self-sentered churches.

At this point I will share some sad facts with you about a church that refused to get involved with missions.

This particular church was founded twelve years ago by a missionary — a missionary sincerely burdened, I am sure, with the need for a Baptist church in a town void of any true gospel witness. The work progressed at a snail's pace, despite the missionary's efforts to reach people through faithful door-to-door visitation. Over a period of several years, a very small nucleus formed, a church was established and eventually a building was erected. Although challenged on every hand by fellow pastors and friends, this missionary absolutely refused to get his church involved with missions.

On a rare occasion a passing missionary was invited to speak. When some of the church folks got a gleam in their eyes and a spark of desire in their hearts to do something for the visiting missionary — the fire was immediately quenched! The excuse? "We need the money here in our own church, **we** need, **we** need, **we** need. . . ." Need I say more?

At the end of ten years, not one missionary had come under the support of that church, not one missionary conference, not one true functioning spark of missions programming! Is it any wonder that the church claimed just the original nucleus plus a few strays at the end of ten years? Yes, there was a beautiful building, but it contained no real church! It was a case of a misled group of believers under the control of a misled pastor. They were sincere, but sincerely wrong.

People involved in a church such as this are love-starved, suffering from the contagious disease known as "malnutrition of the heart"!

Pause here — again, evaluate your missions program!

Now let us check out our teenage years — remember them? Life, enthusiasm, vibrancy — ready to conquer!

It is time to expand your ministry in missions. Enlarge upon your original ten steps.

1. Have your monthly mission Sunday go beyond the pastor's or missionary's messages. Involve the **music ministry.** Occasionally have a mission cantata or group specials to highlight this particular Sunday. Teach mission choruses and songs. Seek out good **mission films** or **slide presentations.** Have the teens present a **mission play.** Draw up one year's schedule of your missions Sundays, and make them very, very special with the idea of reaching and activating every heart in your church for missions.

2. Continue to open your doors to visiting (approved) missionaries. A secure pastor will not fear relinquishing his pulpit. Consider using missionary families to **teach your vacation Bible school** — you cannot overestimate the impact of such an endeavor as this. It really draws your children — and they never forget the week Missionary Bill (or whoever) spent with them.

3. Drop the "mini" — and have a **real conference.** (Conference and missions support are covered elsewhere in the book.)

4. Expand the visual impact from your **bulletin board** to include the tract rack, magazine periodicals (provided by mission boards upon request), weekly bulletins, monthly newsletters, prayer flyers, etc.

5. You may want to prepare for **mission prayer bands** in your church. Have head prayer warriors meet with groups of people in the same age bracket to pray especially for specific missionaries or specific fields.

6. The **mission file** should be reviewed *annually* by the pastor and missions committee. Do not bypass any area of the missionaries' letters, needs, cost of living increases, etc. Keep a watchful eye on your missionaries! It may take time, but it is imperative that you check regularly on your missionary's beliefs, associations on the field, and his production. (Some missionaries consider their term on the field as a nice paid vacation. No kidding! Be alert!!)

Expect a report (even request it) from every missionary under support. How many souls have been added to his account through your mission support? Also, check out his doctrinal stand — this has been known to change once the missionary is isolated from strong believers and exposed to "friendly" neo-evangelicals.

7. As you keep up with your home church **photo album,** share some of your church blessings with the missionaries. Send them an occasional snapshot of a special social or some unusual event to keep them in touch with your activities. Good communication is a two-way street.

8. After your Sunday School classes have a good foundation for missions, start having monthly **mission projects.** These may be done by individual classes or the Sunday School departments as a whole. (Projects need to be coordinated and promoted.) You will find projects reviewed more fully in another chapter.

9. Have your correspondence encompass more than just sending **birthday** and **anniversary cards.** Encourage your people to write letters. You may even want to supply preaddressed aerograms.

10. **Christmas gifts** . . . your first year may be enough to whet the appetites of your people to look further into establishing the Ladies' Missionary Fellowship — a big plus if organized and executed properly.

As your church progresses through your teenage growth, you will surely have increased your missions budget. **This budget should include only the support of missionaries and special gifts for them!** Your Christian day school, bus ministry, tape ministry, deaf ministry, benevolent ministry, tract ministry are all an integral part of "home base" — *the local church* — and, therefore, should be incorporated into your General Fund — *not* into missions! (Christian day schools usually operate under their own treasury.)

Many a good missions program has been thwarted by the selfish cry of those who throw every ministry ingredient into the mission pot. Thus missions loses its own flavor and becomes a wishy-washy nothingness. This is why missionaries (those called of God for a particular purpose — missions) are not able to raise their initial support to get out onto the field!

These points about the budget may stagger some of you, so take a break here and really think about what has been said. For those who have become a little hot under the collar, relax — sift through some of the Scriptures relating to missions and pray about your own feelings on the subject.

Some may say, "We are all missionaries." This is a cop-out to work around their idea of incorporating every ministry into the missions budget. We all should have a particular ministry in the local church, but we do not divide the spoils every Sunday among ourselves.

Once you get some surefootedness under the teenage years of your church, you are then ready for the maturity in your missions program — the Adult Years. Oh, the blessings awaiting that glorious, glowing, growing missionary-minded church!

...

3
Missions
and the adult church

At **this point** in your church growth in missions, you should be sensitive to the complete (mature) cycle of mission activity that can be attained in the local church.

There will be a oneness of spirit among the people of your church as they regard the full impact of 2 Corinthians 2:14–17.

> Now thanks be unto God, which always causeth us to triumph in Christ, and maketh manifest the savour of his knowledge by us in every place.
> For we are unto God a sweet savour of Christ, in them that are saved, and in them that perish:
> To the one we are the savour of death unto death; and to the other the savour of life unto life. And who is sufficient for these things?
> For we are not as many, which corrupt the word of God: but as of sincerity, but as of God, in the sight of God speak we in Christ.

The pastor will have thoroughly taught and prepared his people to have compassionate hearts in response to any phase of mission programming which is presented to them.

Because of the spiritual condition of the healthy adult church, the teaching process must always continue. Why? A mature church will have a goodly number of new converts, ones who may never have heard the word "missions." The healthy church will continually be in the business of training.

For those who see the years passing swiftly by, this

teaching and training process is becoming a matter of utmost importance. There is a keen awareness and urgency to see the propagation of good mission programming handed down to "prepared" followers.

In addition to the ten steps listed under the young church and the teenage church, you may choose to add some of the following steps to your ladder of success.

1. Include **training sessions** in missions among the courses offered at the adult workshops on Sunday evenings. Encourage all Sunday School teachers, deacons, officers, and youth leaders to attend.

2. Involve your **tape ministry** as a means of communication between you and your missionaries. Tape occasional church specials which might be an encouragement to the missionary on the field. Send a church-family letter on tape to each missionary under support. This was very well received by missionaries of one particular church:

> The church family met for its Annual Watchnight Fellowship. During the refreshment hour each family entered one at a time, into a room which had been set up for the purpose of taping this letter. Some families shared personal happenings of their children, special blessings of the past year, encouragement for the year ahead, jokes and tall tales about hunting, etc. The closing portion was by the pastor — he ended on a serious thought and prayer for the missionaries as they labored in their various fields. Copies of the tape were made, with one being sent to each missionary.

3. The successful Ladies' Missionary Fellowship may plant some seeds of thought in the hearts of the men and young people of the church. They, too, may desire to launch out into a special **missions fellowship** drawn up and geared to their particular abilities.

4. **Visit** supported missionaries on their respective fields! What an encouragement this is to a missionary — and what an education for the visitor! It is one of the most effective tools used to increase the vision of any local church. See that your pastor is gifted with such a trip!

5. As the word gets out about the great missions out-reach of your church, the pastor will be flooded with **mail** from hopeful missionaries. Unfortunately, not all mission-aries can fit into your church schedule or your church bud-get. (Note: Not all are taken on for financial support — but they can receive a one-time love gift and a promise of prayer.) As your church continues to grow, missionaries should be included in your youth programs, rallies, Sunday Schools, socials, ladies' fellowships, men's prayer break-fasts, Bible clubs, rest home ministries, etc.

Your church may be doing many things over-and-above the aforementioned suggestions, Praise the Lord!

Now to wrap up the three stages of church growth, the real test of a missionary-minded church is:

A. How many new works have come as a direct result of the ministry of your church?
B. How many young people are away at Christian colleges preparing for full-time Christian service?
C. How many missionaries have been commis-sioned and sent forth from your membership?

We are not an entity unto ourselves. We, too, must propagate.

4
Our ministry

Pray ye therefore, the Lord of the harvest, that He would raise up church members to love, support, to uphold in prayer, to work for the labourers who have been sent into His Harvest Fields.

Christ went to Calvary **for us,** in our stead — He took our place. He was **One sent** of God for a purpose!

*   *   *   *   *   *   *   *   *   *   *   *   *

SUNDAY SCHOOL TEACHERS:

Take five minutes each week for missions.

Have a missionary map in your classroom (yarn and pin locations).

Have pictures of supported missionaries and biography of each.

Use mission songs and choruses.

Letter-a-month — have your class write to a missionary each month.

Send cards and notes for holidays, birthdays, anniversaries.

Visit area missionaries as a field trip.

Encourage daily prayer for missionaries.

Read prayer letters with your class.

Have a mission library — books to loan out in your class.

Have slides and films on missions.

Send gifts from your class to missionaries.

Encourage pupils to earn and save money for the missionary cupboard.

Give homework assignments to study and report on culture, geography and religion of different countries.

Use "Around the World" socials for your class — include decorations, costumes, foods, films from other countries.

SOCIAL
COMMITTEE: A great "in" for pushing missions.

The committee usually should plan a year in advance for monthly adult fellowship meetings — invite your missionary well in advance. (Check to see if the missionary can stay over to speak on the following Sunday.)

Include missionary guests in your activities — such as a Hawaiian Luau, Spaghetti Bash, Beach Party, Turkey Dinner, Christmas Party. (They like volleyball games, parties, swimming, bowling, food and fellowships, too.)

Ask them to share their testimonies, work, and a devotional. This is a good opportunity to help folks relate to missionaries in an informal atmosphere.

CHURCH
SECRETARY: Push missions in your weekly church bulletin. Use Scripture verses, news from the field, portions of prayer letters, quotes and poems.

Publish monthly mission flyers.

Maintain and update bulletin boards.

Keep mission **tracts** in the tract rack.

Keep an adequate number of periodicals from mission boards on hand for each church family.

YOUTH
LEADERS: Take one meeting a month for missions — some groups even include long range plans to visit mission fields in other parts of the country, or even the world (encourage

them to earn money for this).

Have a **Teen Work Night for Missions** — use your Ladies' Missionary Fellowship to head up and direct each endeavor (this will prevent overlapping of projects and possible problems). Some groups make flannelgraph scenes, cut out flannelgraph stories, make wordless books, scrapbooks, collect and prepare greeting cards to fit the missionary's specifications, make quilts, save Green Stamps, save Betty Crocker coupons and purchase particular items.

Use mission films, records and speakers whenever possible.

LIBRARIANS: If your church does not have a library, ask your pastor's permission to set up a **Missions Lending Library.** Books should be "screened" by someone before being placed on the shelves. This will prevent new believers from becoming confused by the many "off-beat" publications.

PHOTO-
GRAPHERS: Take pictures and keep an album of visiting missionaries. Make this very neat and artistic and let it be part of your church display.

ARTISTS: If you can print, draw or paint — volunteer. Your services may be of great value to your church missions committee in preparing posters, banners, flyers and booklets for conferences or general publicity.

TAPE
RECORDERS: Have one? Great! Offer your services to record each missionary speaker who comes to your church. Keep a tape library — share them with shut-ins.

Tape your pastor's messages, your choir, your young people, and mail a tape to your missionaries.

HOME-MAKERS: **Hospitality** — Open your home. Volunteer to feed and lodge visiting missionaries. This will be a great blessing to you and your family and you will be a blessing to the missionary, too.

Preconference Prayer Meetings — Open your home for prayer.

Groceries — Buy and prepare foods for hostesses who are lodging missionaries. (If you had a dozen people for breakfast, wouldn't you like to have some church folks send in bacon, eggs, juice, bread?)

Conference Bible Studies — Open your home to neighborhood women. Invite them over for an hour of visiting with missionaries and ask one missionary to present a study from God's Word.

Babysitting — Offer your services. Some young mother might like to relax and receive a blessing and challenge. (Many times we shoo our teens out to cope with the baby situation — what a sad mistake. How many future missionaries get lost along the way among the diapers and baby bottles.)

Telephoning — Extend personal invitations to conference sessions.

Encourage your family to share in the whirlwind preparations for visiting missionaries. Let daughter bake — let son help the missionary change the oil or wash his car — let husband visit with missionary (ahem . . . without your supervision).

PRO-FESSIONALS: Mechanics, printers, machinists, doctors, opticians, dentists, nurses, etc. — whatever your profession, volunteer your services in whatever way possible to assist the missionary.

PRAYER WARRIORS:	"God forbid that I should sin against the Lord in ceasing to pray for you" . . . we can ALL pray!
	Keep your missionaries' physical and spiritual needs before the Throne of Grace daily.

ELECTED POSITIONS:

Missions Committee

Qualifications — *Called* of God — Willing to *sacrifice* — Spiritually *mature* — Have a *vision* for missions.

Each member of the committee should have an active part in keeping missions before the church — training, educating and encouraging TOTAL church involvement.

The key person is the pastor . . . he must lead the way! If a pastor holds back and is not sincerely enthusiastic in presenting the missions program, the people sense this and will NOT cooperate.

Missionary speakers on a regular basis, plus a well-planned Missionary Conference, are a MUST for your church.

*   *   *   *   *   *   *   *   *   *   *   *   *

Recommended Reading: *Missionary Administration in the Local Church* by Reginald L. Matthews, D.D.
Women's World Handbook by Dorothy Vander Kaay.

PART 2

Conferences

5
Conferences: burdens and blessings

And when they had ordained them elders in every church, and had prayed with fasting, they commended them to the Lord, on whom they believed.
And after they had passed throughout Pisidia, they came to Pamphylia.
And when they had preached the word in Perga, they went down into Attalia.
And thence sailed to Antioch, from whence they had been recommended to the grace of God for the work which they fulfilled.
*And when they were come, and had gathered the church together, **they rehearsed all that God had done with them,** and how he had opened the door of faith unto the Gentiles.*
And there they abode long time with the disciples (Acts 14:23–28).

* * * * * * * * * * * * * *

The **above portion** of Scripture should be reason enough to have an Annual Missionary Conference. Our churches need to be opened to God's servants so that they might have the opportunity to report the mission activity on their particular field. In turn, God's people are given the opportunity to respond to the challenge from each missionary and from each field.

The "burden" of the Annual Missionary Conference falls on the shoulders of the mission committee. (This is a joyous burden to those who have hearts geared for missions.) To have a well-planned conference, the task of organizing must begin at least ten months before the set dates of the conference. Do not allow your conference to be a last minute after-thought — "Well, I guess we should have a missionary conference . . . see who's in the area (we don't want to spend more than we have to on travel expenses) . . . give them a few days at the end of the month . . . and, a-h-h-h, we'll see what happens." Such statements as these should never be made about this most important ministry as expounded from God's Word! We need to shed tears over those in leadership positions in our local churches who have such an apathetic attitude towards missions!

The first step towards a successful conference is to remember that GOD ALONE is the only One Who can give you the conference you desire for your church. You must **pray** about every phase of your conference.

Some guidelines you may want to consider:

PHASE 1

1. Set the *dates*. Conferences used to be an October or April affair, but many churches now are using November ("harvest") or February ("heart").

2. Determine the *length* of the conference. Most young and teen-age churches will go Wednesday through Sunday, or Saturday through Wednesday.

3. What *type* of conference? One field represented, one board represented, or a mixture?

4. *How many* missionaries? A good rule of thumb is to invite only as many missionaries as you have conference days — *NO MORE!* There will not be enough time for proper exposure of each missionary and it is stifling for the missionary and confusing for the people!

5. *Which* missionaries? *Where* can I find them? Most mission boards publish a quarterly "deputation listing" for the

purpose of assisting churches in their search for guest speakers. Seriously consider the value of including both veteran and appointee missionaries. They each have much to share — the one experience and the other enthusiasm!

As soon as you decide which route to take, contact the missionary. The missionaries need to have advance notice to help them in coordinating their deputation itinerary.

You will probably need a list of twelve suggested missionary speakers before actually settling on the four you need. Trust the Lord to bring in the confirmations — this may sound difficult, especially when you are anxious to firm-up your conference. He never fails! Just keep going down your list of twelve and be patient!

6. Decide on a conference *theme!* There are many "gimmick" types of themes that are acceptable but only if you include a Scripture verse to go along with them. Do not neglect God's Word to promote God's Work!

7. Determine your conference *goals* — very important! What do you desire to see accomplished in the lives of your people as a result of this conference?

8. *Money!* A successfully planned conference will have all financial bases covered before the opening night of the conference. Things to be considered are: missionary travel expenses to and from your conference (figure the mileage), a kick-off banquet, a generous church gift for each missionary. How can this be accomplished beforehand? Step out on faith with your people! Three months before the conference, your pastor may bring a challenge on missions and preconference faith promise pledges.

A small church was planning its third missionary conference when the idea of preconference giving was introduced. A slip of paper was given out and people prayed concerning their part in this particular conference. No names were to be written, just amounts. The pledge made by the people was to give $1,000 over an eight week period before the conference. By the first meeting, all expenses were met and the total of $1,300 was in the treasury for *the missionaries. (Also several personal monetary gifts were given by individuals.)*

One young mother of six children gave testimony of how God had brought in the exact amount of money she had pledged for the conference. Tears of joy ran down her face as she told of God's faithfulness. Her only job was waitressing at night at Papa Gino's Pizza Place.

No debts should be accrued from your conference! In fact, a conference is the ideal time to consider your yearly faith-promise to missions. There will be some very strong feelings injected at this point! As your church adopts the faith-promise plan for giving to missions, *do not* tie up missions funds from one conference to the next! Some churches will not consider taking missionaries on for support during the twelve months in between — this is ridiculous! A missionary should not have to wait indefinitely to see if a church is ready to take on such support. A quarterly review of missionary speakers is a fair method for all concerned.

PHASE II

You have the dates, the type of conference, the number and names of accepted missionaries and the conference theme. Now:

1. Prepare a *Preconference Prayer Booklet*, which includes one page of information on each conference speaker. On each page have a map of the field, the missionary's address, birthday, anniversary, family birthdays, type of ministry involvement, and personal prayer requests. Make this booklet as attractive and informative as possible, and give it out to the people six weeks before the conference. Encourage "family prayer" in the homes for the conference speakers.

2. Formulate two types of promotional contests — a poster contest and an essay contest.

3. Plan for Preconference Prayer Meetings — one a week for six weeks prior to the conference. If your church

is large, there may be the need for several homes to be opened for prayer each week.

PHASE III

1. Final confirmation of arrival dates and times, the conference schedule, a map, and a note of encouragement should be mailed to each missionary at least three weeks before conference dates.

2. Have lodging all arranged for missionaries, plus post a sign-up list for evening meals.

3. You may want to use the contest posters to line your hallways for promotional purposes.

4. Prepare newspaper and radio announcements.

5. Have as much completed before the conference week as you possibly can. You will need to be physically rested and spiritually prepared to receive the many blessings which the Lord will have for you.

6. Sometime during your conference *make time* to interview each missionary separately, making sure that your spirit does not strive against the missionary's spirit. Reaffirm that you have no ecclesiastical differences, and check out the missionary's life and goals.

7. Meet as a committee to evaluate your conference! Were your goals attained? If not — why not?

To encourage you, let me tell you the story of a successful local church.

This work started in a home eleven years ago by a pastor new to this section of the country. He faced the culture shock of any southerner relocating in New England. But his faith did not waiver and he proceeded to set about to do the work to which he had been called, establishing a fundamental Baptist church.

From the onset of the work, missions played an important part in this church. God supplied in a great way as

37

property was provided, a building erected, special ministries developed, a day care center, Christian day school up through grade twelve, and a college — all in eleven years.

How could this happen in such a short time? This church is under the leadership of a dedicated, God-fearing, compassionate pastor with a heart for missions. These traits are reflected in many of the lives of people in various church ministries. An attitude of love is shown among the people.

A current update in the missions program of this church shows a faith-promise of $56,000 with thirty-four missionaries under support, promotional materials on display, deacons keeping records of missionary reports and correspondence, and the ladies preparing for next year's conference gifts. The pastor is careful to interview every missionary who enters his pulpit.

The slogan for the Christian day school during a week in February was "It makes sense to give cents to missions." The high schoolers brought in all the pennies they had to help pay for a missionary's barrels. They collected $275 in pennies.

Above these involvements, the church has had direct influence on the propagation of at least five new works. The Lord's hand of blessing is truly upon this work.

Faithful is he that calleth you,
who also will do it (1 Thess. 5:24).

CONFERENCE POSTER CONTEST RULES

(Sample)

1. Three divisions:
    Juniors — grades 4, 5, 6
    Teens
    Adults

2. Poster must be on ½ of a piece of posterboard, any color.

3. Our conference theme *must* appear on the poster, and the pictures and drawings should illustrate the theme. Include dates.

4. Posters will be judged on originality, use of theme and neatness.

5. Name must be written on the *back* of the poster.

6. Posters must be turned in no later than ___(date)___. They should be placed in the Sunday School office.

7. Judges will be the visiting missionaries.

8. Crayons, magic markers, poster paints and hand cut lettering may be used.

9. *Prizes* will be awarded at the close of the conference.

10. Posters turned in will be displayed throughout the church during the conference.

11. The work you turn in must *be your own* — no assistance from parents or friends.
    - ** Start thinking today!
    - ** Begin collecting pictures.
    - ** Make it a family affair — moms and dads, too.
    - ** Teachers . . . plan a poster party for your class.
    - ** Grades 1, 2, 3 will have a coloring contest. Missionaries will be judges and prizes will be awarded.

ESSAY CONTEST RULES *(Sample)*

1. For grades 6–12.
2. Write between 250-350 words on 8½ x 11 lined paper.
3. Topic: Your thoughts on the conference theme.

4. Essays will be judged on content and neatness.
5. Missionaries will be the judges.
6. Turn in to your Sunday School teacher by __(date)__ .
7. Winning essay will be read during one of the conference sessions.

6
Conference blunders

Webster defines a *blunder* as an avoidable error.

Beware of conference blunders. . . .
The annual missionary conference is the one set of special meetings which can bring the greatest blessings and most lasting decisions in the local church. These precious results can sometimes be overshadowed by careless blunders among the church people. Here are a few areas to watch.

1. Include as many people as possible in your planning stage. Do not *force* people to participate, but allow for *volunteer* participants. Sign-up lists on the bulletin board or church "service records" are of great benefit in securing workers.

2. Be sure to "clue-in" your host homes on the procedures for preparing for guests. (Some people really do not know how to entertain.) Areas to check: A *clean* bedroom (air it — dust it — and provide clean sheets!), clean towels, tissues, hand lotion, clean water glass, hard candy, aspirin, lamp for reading, clock, and an empty wastebasket. Sounds like you're preparing for royalty! Well, you are! They are the King's messengers!
The rest of your home should be at the missionary's disposal. Make your guest feel welcome — encourage the missionary to slip into comfortable clothes, to join in the family gab session, to walk or work out in your yard, to use the phone, and to snoop in your (clean) refrigerator.

3. Watch out for individuals who decide to "do their own thing" with the visiting missionaries, throwing scheduled plans into a whirlwind. Conferences are not a personal "clique-time" — the missionaries are guests of the *church!*

4. Many times pastors encourage church folks to open their homes for fellowship following conference sessions. If this is the case, then *be sure* to invite at least the family of the "host home" along with the pastor's family. They may not always be able to attend, but be courteous and extend the invitation.

5. Entertaining a missionary for a meal in your home should not give way to "washing the church's linen." (One missionary took part in a rather large "busy" conference. Having been invited into four church homes for meals, this missionary was *deluged* with *four* different gripe sessions by *four* different factions of the church.)

6. The "busy" conference can drain the missionary as well as the church people. Do not run early morning to late evening sessions without a personal free-time, or break. There will be need for showers, laundry, studying, praying, and just plain "feet-up and snooze" time.

7. Don't be a *mole!* No underground manipulation of the church people during the conference, please! If much prayer has gone into your conference, then continue to trust the Lord to direct the decisions of the pastor and missions committee.

8. Remember the *quiet people* — the precious faithful ones who so often are the supportive element behind the assertive missions committee. It is their labors of love which encourage the mainstream of workers to continue faithfully in their service for the Lord. Include these folks in your home fellowships.

Much more could be said, but to summarize the whole area of "blunders" let's remember Paul's words — *Let love be without dissimulation. Abhor that which is evil; cleave to that which is good. Be kindly affectioned one to another with brotherly love; in honour preferring one another (Rom. 12:9, 10).*

MISSIONARY BLUNDERS

Yes, they do make a few. The church is not always at fault in this area.

1. The *T.V.-aholic*. The hostess invites people over after church to fellowship with the missionary, and she has to keep hauling the missionary away from the television.

The *Sportsnut*. After delivering a strong message on dedication, the missionary sends the people home to "think on these things." Then, this very same missionary spends the afternoon with his eyeballs hanging out of the sockets watching the football game (or basketball, or hockey, or baseball, or wrestling). Your young people notice this!

2. The missionary who is participating in your conference — requests to slip away for a few hours to visit friends in a nearby town — and then *forgets* about returning for the next scheduled meeting.

3. The missionary who says he is coming alone and arrives with his wife *and* children.

4. The missionary who gets so involved with *tale-telling* that he does not see his children destroying the host's home.

5. The *sick* children — they arrive at the conference with a communicable disease (leaving the church parents gasping and the hostess burning.)

6. The *misplaced* correspondence — the church waits and waits for replies to letters. Either file "13" has the church's letter, or it is under a heap of other unanswered letters!

7. The missionary who is *undisciplined* and will not even taste foods that are unfamiliar, or are not his/her favorites. Going from home to home is difficult, but it is bad manners to ignore the culinary efforts of the hostess (allergies being the exception).

8. The *slob*! (My, what a crass thing to say!) Some missionaries do not know how to be guests — never make a bed, never lift a dish, throw dirty clothes in a heap on the floor, and display habits only suitable for the privacy of their own home.

43

9. The *prankster!* It's one thing to invite a missionary to snoop in your refrigerator; but, it's another thing for the missionary to snoop in daughter's dresser. Then, to take all her pantyhose and tie them in knots, remove the support from one corner of the bed, and break her clock-radio by setting it to go off at 3:00 A.M. (as a joke). Some things just aren't funny!

Yes, our missionaries do make blunders — none of which should discourage the church people from loving them.

> *Wherefore let him that thinketh he standeth take heed lest he fall (1 Cor. 10:12).*
> *But let patience have her perfect work, that ye may be perfect and entire, wanting nothing (James 1:4).*

44

7
Conference schedules

The following are samples of very simple conference schedules, ones which can be added to very easily. Do not forget your teens — set aside one time during the conference for them. *Do not* have your schedules so involved that an interpreter is needed.

SAMPLE 1

. . . Pray Ye Therefore the Lord of the Harvest, that He Would Send Forth Labourers into His Harvest . . . Luke 10:2

Date _____

Thursday ____	7:30 P.M.	Slides: Missionary #4
		Panel: "The Indigenous Church Policy"
		Message: Missionary #2
Friday ____	10:00 A.M.	Coffee Hour with all missionaries
		Discussion and Questions: Missions In The Home
	7:30 P.M.	Slides: Missionary #3
		Panel: "Education of Missionary Children"
		Message: Missionary #1

Saturday _____	8:00 A.M.	Men's Prayer Breakfast
	12:00 P.M.	Lunch: Teens and Missionaries
	1:00 P.M.	Teen Roundtable Discussion on "The Call to the Mission Field"
	6:00 P.M.	Ham and Bean Supper
	7:30 P.M.	Slides: Missionary #2
		Panel: "How to Have a Missionary-Minded Church"
		Message: Missionary #3

Sunday _____	8:00 A.M.	Men's Prayer
	9:15 A.M.	Sunday School:
		Adults—Missionary #1
		Teens—Missionary #2
		Juniors—Missionary #3
		Primary—Missionary #4
	10:30 A.M.	Morning Worship
		Message: Missionary #4
	6:00 P.M.	Mission Workshop: "Cults"
		Missionary #3
	7:00 P.M.	Slides: Missionary #1
		Message: Missionary #2

**Testimonies   Special Music   Slides
Curios   Seminars   Messages   Fellowship**

Name   and   Board

Missionary #1
Missionary #2
Missionary #3
Missionary #4

(Conference Logo)

Church Names _____
Church Address _____
Church Phone _____
Host Pastor _____

46

SAMPLE 2

SPRING MISSIONARY
CONFERENCE

APRIL 25—29

_____ BAPTIST CHURCH

_____(Address)_____

UNTOLD MILLIONS ARE STILL UNTOLD

WEDNESDAY — APRIL 25

"Get-Acquainted" Fellowship Supper
(For the Whole Family)

TESTIMONIES: All Missionaries   CHALLENGE: Pastor _____

TIME: 6:00 P.M.   *RESERVATIONS:* _____

THURSDAY
Church 3:30 P.M.
"AROUND THE
WORLD PARTY"
(Primary — Junior)
All Missionaries

FRIDAY
Church 1:00 P.M.
LADIES' MEETING

SATURDAY
Parsonage
        12:00 P.M.
TEEN LUNCHEON

"ROUNDTABLE"
        2:00 P.M.
All Missionaries

BASKETBALL
(Teens vs. Adults)

SUNDAY
Sunday School
        9:45 A.M.
PRIMARY/JUNIOR
    Missionary #2
JR./SR. HIGH
    Missionary #3
ADULTS
    Missionary #1

WORSHIP SERVICE
        11:00 A.M.
Missionary #4

47

7:00 P.M.	7:00 P.M.	7:00 P.M.	7:00 P.M.
SLIDES	SLIDES	SLIDES	SLIDES
Missionary #1	Missionary #4	Missionary #2	Missionary #3
"PANEL"	"PANEL"	"PANEL"	"PANEL"
Missionary #3	Missionary #2	Missionary #4	Missionary #1

MISSIONARY   (Name)   (Board)

"ARISE — GO — PREACH"

SAMPLE 3

"What! Me a Missionary?"

APRIL 1 — 5, 19_____

ANNUAL MISSIONARY CONFERENCE

(Church Name and Address)

SLIDES — CURIOS — SEMINARS — TESTIMONIES

Participating Missionaries (Name — Field — Board of Each)
(#1 — #4)

Saturday, April 1, 5:30 P.M.

AROUND THE WORLD SMORGASBORD
(Adult Fellowship)
TESTIMONIES & THEME CHALLENGE — MISSIONARIES

SUNDAY	MONDAY	TUESDAY	WEDNESDAY
9:45 A.M.	**Pray**	10:30 A.M.	**Pray**
Primaries #3	**Visit**	*Ladies'*	**Visit**
Juniors #2		*Fellowship*	
Teens #1	**Invite**		**Invite**
Adults #4			
11:00 A.M.	7:00 P.M.	7:00 P.M.	
"Personality	Focus #3	Focus #1	7:00 P.M.
Spotlight"	Message #4	Message #2	Focus #4
Message #3			Message #3
5:00 P.M.			* * * *
Seminar			Cupboard
6:00 P.M.			"Shopping"
Focus #2			
Message #1			
8:00 P.M.			
Teen —			
Fellowship			

Displays may be seen following all evening services
Fellowship Room #3.
*Preservice **prayer** will be held in Room #9 before **each service**.*

HOST PASTOR: **PHONE:**

49

For the *young church* — one that is actively engaged in a building program and is concerned that the people are educated and involved in a good missions program, this first conference is very special.

As The Church Grows
✿ So Grows Missions

WED.	THURS.	FRI.
7:00 Get Acquainted Night Testimonies:- Ours & Theirs Challenge- Pastor Refreshments	7:00 Focus Africa Message #1	7:00 Focus Canada Message #2
SAT. 9:00 (A week earlier)* 6:00 Family Supper "M.H.S." **** Cupboard Shopping	SUN. 10:00 S.S. Hour Adult #1 Teen #2 Junior (Wife) #1 Primary (Wife) #2 11:00 Message Guest ** Conference Closes.	"THE HARVEST TRULY IS PLENTEOUS, BUT THE LABOURERS ARE FEW." ✿ - Matt. 9:37

(*A Men's Prayer Breakfast to be held a week before the conference. Use a layman in the church to share his thoughts on missions, a man who has been blessed by such involvement. Have men bring in a "man's gift" to the breakfast — to be placed in the missionary cupboard.)

(***"M.H.S." — Mission Hot Seat. Missionaries will answer questions of the people.)

The harvest truly is plenteous, but the labourers are few (Matt. 9:37).

GUEST SPEAKERS:
   MISSIONARY #1
   MISSIONARY #2
   **AREA PASTOR
   HOST PASTOR

CHURCH NAME & ADDRESS

MISSIONARY RECORD SHEET
(For the Single Missionary)

I. NAME _____ BIRTHDATE _____

   HOME ADDRESS _____ PHONE _____

   FIELD ADDRESS _____ PHONE _____

   HOME CHURCH _____ PHONE _____

   NEAREST RELATIVE _____ PHONE _____

II. EDUCATION:

HIGH SCHOOL _____ GRADUATION _____

COLLEGE _____ GRADUATION _____

SEMINARY _____ GRADUATION _____

SPECIALIZED TRAINING _____

III. GIVE PERSONAL TESTIMONY OF SALVATION (separate sheet)

BAPTISM _____

GIVE PERSONAL TESTIMONY OF CALL TO MISSIONARY SERVICE (separate sheet)

Commissioned at _____ Date _____

Ordained at _____ Date _____

IV. INDICATE STAND ON:

PERSONAL SEPARATION _____

_____

ECCLESIASTICAL SEPARATION _____

_____

Attach the doctrinal statement, principles and practices, and associations of your mission board.

V. FORMER MISSIONARY SERVICE (if any):

BOARD _____ DATES From _____ to _____

FIELD _____

Reason for leaving this board _____

_____

History of your service with present mission board _____

_____

Describe the work you will do on your current field _____

_____

DATE NEXT FURLOUGH IS DUE _____ ENDING _____

VI. MAILING SPECIFICATIONS (Field):

LIST PERSONAL NEEDS:

Item   **Size**   **Color**   **Material**

MISCELLANEOUS HOUSEHOLD ITEMS:

Item   **Description**

FIELD SUPPLIES:

Item   **Description**

VII. PLEASE ATTACH A CURRENT PHOTOGRAPH. THANK YOU FOR YOUR COOPERATION.

Note: This same record sheet may be used for the missionary couple. Additional information you will want: names and birthdates of children along with their needs and sizes.

PART 3

Projects

8
Projects

Now ye Philippians know also, that in the beginning of the gospel, when I departed from Macedonia, no church communicated with me as concerning giving and receiving, but ye only. For even in Thessalonica ye sent once and again unto my necessity. Not because I desire a gift: but I desire fruit that may abound to your account (Phil. 4:15–17).

* * * * * * * * * * * * *

The above portion of Scripture should be enough to spur us on to do all we can to help our missionaries.

PROJECTS. These can be broken down into three categories:

1. **Ladies' Missionary Work Projects**
2. **Sunday School Class Projects**
3. **All-Church Projects**

There needs to be a sweet spirit among the church people in order for these various projects to be God-honoring! Unless these are well-coordinated by your missions committee, problems could arise.

A good line of delegations should be set up at the onset of such endeavors in the local church. Ideas need to be hashed over, prayed about, and determined by your missions committee. Since the Ladies' Missionary Fellowship is aware of the current mission needs, the president of this group would be a great asset to the missions committee.

After projects are approved, they should be thoroughly explained at the Sunday School Teachers

57

Meeting — there should be no doubt about the type of project and how it is to be executed. Teachers need to be supportive of the mission work in order to properly promote it in their Sunday School classes. (If a Sunday School teacher hinders the project or shows other evidences that she is not missionary-minded, there should be serious doubt as to whether that person is qualified to teach at all.)

PROJECT DROP-OFF. Prepare a particular location for placing finished projects. A large barrel with a world map wrapped around it is good or an old fashioned trunk with the raised lid lined with a world map is another idea. Make the area special and attractive to the eye.

PROJECT DISPERSEMENT. Some projects will be prepared to meet the needs of a particular missionary either under present support or coming to visit.

Other projects will be placed in the missionary cupboard to be given out to visiting missionaries throughout the year or to be used at the annual missionary conference.

The Ladies' Missionary Fellowship will oversee the maintenance of the missionary cupboard and will keep an accurate inventory list. It is advisable to see that the pastor has a duplicate list of the items in the missionary cupboard. Also, keep the lines of communication open between the pastor and the ladies lest there be any misunderstandings. Some pastors are so bogged down with "important" matters that a small thing like the missionary cupboard seems unimportant. Many a forest fire has been started by the little spark of misunderstanding. These misunderstandings can discourage pastors and/or ladies from asserting any enthusiasm for missions in their church. If your pastor brushes aside your attempts to share every phase of the work with him, keep after him until you get his attention. This will save many a heartache!

FINAL THOUGHT. On the following pages are sample flyers which have been used to promote mission projects. Give flyers out well in advance of the due date. This will allow your people to take advantage of the items they can find on sale — then they can buy all the more!

SAMPLE 1

MARCH
W
I
T
H
MISSIONS

SUNDAY #1

Help "Sew-Up" the holes
in the
Missionary Cupboard
Bring in THREAD...
all colors!

SUNDAY #2

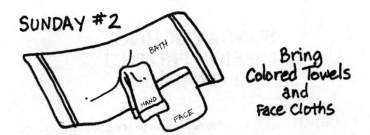

BATH

HAND

FACE

Bring
Colored Towels
and
Face Cloths

59

SUNDAY #3

Scrub-a-dub-dub....
Put DIAL in the tub...

Bring in DIAL soap-all sizes!

SUNDAY #4

Help us *fill up* with
Saran Wrap · Kleenex · Bathroom Tissue
Glad Bags · Paper Towels · Note Paper · Gift Wrap

SAMPLE 2

SUNDAY SCHOOL
MISSION PROJECT
FOR APRIL

On April 22 Rev. Charles Anderson will be our guest speaker for the morning and evening hours. Rev. Anderson will be presenting the mission work in France. At that time we would like to fulfill some of his needs. The Sunday School classes are being asked to help with this project.

ADULTS:	Money for subscriptions to:
	Good Housekeeping
	Camping Guide
	Ladies Home Journal
	Better Homes and Gardens
	Books:
	Children's books
	Christian novels — Adult
	Missionary stories — Adult
	Socks:
	Men's size 11
	Boys' sizes 8 and 5½ — cotton or orlon
	Undershirts:
	Boys' sizes 5 and 2 — white, cotton, short sleeves
HIGH SCHOOL:	Attendance cards — 300 (50 of each picture)
	Religious pictures (flat card type for awards)
JUNIOR HIGH:	Construction paper — 10 packs of assorted colors
JUNIORS:	Pencils with Scripture verses on them
	Stickers (birds, flowers, stars, crosses, Bibles) 100 packs
PRIMARIES:	Bookmarks with Scripture verses
BEGINNERS:	Cake mixes — frosting mixes — puddings
ALL CLASSES:	Christmas cards with backs neatly cut off
	Used picture postcards
	All sorts of colored magazine pictures

Please, bring these items in to your class on *April 1, 8, or 15.* Presentation of these gifts will be made to Rev. Anderson during the Sunday School Hour on April 22.

Come with us to

BRAZIL

AREA-WIDE LADIES' RALLY

APRIL 25, 19_____ AT _____ BAPTIST CHURCH

Time: 10:00 A.M. — 2:00 P.M. (Registration at 9:45 A.M.)
Guest Speaker: Miss Agnes Haik — Missionary to Brazil — A.B.W.E.

Schedule

9:45 - Registration

10:00 - Welcome . . . Songs . . . Prayer

Workshop . . . *In the Word* . . . Miss Haik

12:00 - Lunch

1:00 - Song . . . Offering
To the Field . . . Miss Haik
CHALLENGE/SLIDES/
QUESTIONS

KID'S CORNER:
A Children's Hour in the morning for all up to age 6.
Bring a sandwich for your child.
Beverage and dessert provided.

BABY NURSERY

RESERVATIONS MUST BE MAILED BY APRIL 18th.

Shower
Since Miss Haik cannot be in each church during this furlough, there will be a shower for her. If you can bring any of the following items, please do so.

Note paper
Stamps
Tupperware — large storage pieces
Shampoo — toothpaste — Kleenex
Paper towels — Saran Wrap — toilet paper
Coke — Pringles — travel snacks
Towels — face cloths — dish towels
Double bed sheets — pillow cases
Size 7 "scuffs"
Sleeveless knit shells
Sleeveless nighties
Jean Nate toiletries

July Mission Project

The special project for July involves bringing in the needed items for D.V.B.S. at mission churches.

They may be brought in any Sunday during July and placed in the boxes out in the north wing.

Miscellaneous
Cold drink cups
Packaged cookies
Large cans of Kool Aid
Napkins
Paper towels

Beginners
Crayons
Elmer's Glue
Construction paper

Kindergarten
Crayola crayons
Play-Doh
Craft sticks
Animal seals
Assorted color felt squares
5 shoe boxes
Plastic bottles (100 aspirin size)
Half pint milk cartons
Aluminum pie plates
Cottage cheese containers

Primaries
60 6 oz. juice cans
60 small plastic butter tubs
60 pencils
60 pair moveable eyes
60 potted plant slips
Large container of old crayons
Colorful contact paper

Juniors
40 6" x 8" of ¼ wood
40 quart plastic containers
   (bleach, milk, juice)
 1 can spray varnish
 8 large-eyed yarn needles
20 assorted colors — felt
 2 pkgs. silver stars
40 pencils
15 small Elmer's Glue
   Rug yarn - assorted colors
   (2 of each color)

Every Sunday School class is taking part in this important project . . . The mission churches have been broken down by classes in order that you may know the needs of each D.V.B.S. department. The Lord bless you as you give.

Pantry Shower for

<u>(Name of missionary)</u>

NURSERY — BEGINNER — PRIMARY

Napkins	Baggies	Scouring pads
Paper towels	Saran Wrap	Paper plates
Reynolds Wrap	Detergent	Hot/cold cups
Wax paper	Soap	T.P./Kleenex

JUNIORS — JUNIOR HIGH — SENIOR HIGH

Tuna fish	Cranberry Sauce	Peanut butter
Spam	Walnuts	Marshmellow fluff
Spaghetti	Raisins	Cereals
Macaroni	Dates	Pickles

ADULTS

Apples	Flour	Miracle Whip
Onions	Salad oil	Salt/pepper
Squash	Potatoes	Mustard
Canned Veg's	Sugar	Ketchup

NOVEMBER

SUNDAY SCHOOL PROJECT

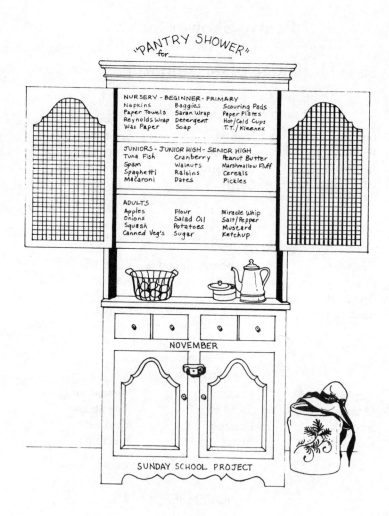

"PANTRY SHOWER"
for_____

NURSERY - BEGINNER - PRIMARY

Napkins	Baggies	Scouring Pads
Paper Towels	Saran Wrap	Paper Plates
Reynolds Wrap	Detergent	Hot/Cold Cups
Wax Paper	Soap	T.T./Kleenex

JUNIORS - JUNIOR HIGH - SENIOR HIGH

Tuna Fish	Cranberry	Peanut Butter
Spam	Walnuts	Marshmallow Fluff
Spaghetti	Raisins	Cereals
Macaroni	Dates	Pickles

ADULTS

Apples	Flour	Miracle Whip
Onions	Salad Oil	Salt/Pepper
Squash	Potatoes	Mustard
Canned Veg's	Sugar	Ketchup

NOVEMBER

SUNDAY SCHOOL PROJECT

PART 4

Studies

STUDY
MATERIAL #1

Many times when we embark upon the road of teaching in Sunday School, daily vacation Bible school, Bible clubs, and Youth meetings, we find that the teachers do not know *why* missions should be included or *how* missions could be included.

Guidelines for Teaching Missions could be used as part of teacher-training workshops. This study material was drawn up specifically for a daily vacation Bible school training session.

GUIDELINES FOR TEACHING MISSIONS

I. *Self-examination*

1. Am I missionary minded?
2. Do I know what a missionary is?
3. Do I know where to locate "The Great Commission" in the Bible?
4. Do I know the names and locations of our church missionaries?
5. Do I pray for missions?
6. Do I give to missions?
7. Would I be willing to say "yes" if God called me to be a missionary?
8. Do I really understand the subject I will be teaching?
9. Am I a "lesson presenter" or a teacher?

Your heart and head must be "full" in order to adequately teach missions.

You **cannot** teach what you **do not** know!

What is your **goal** in teaching missions? Are you using missions as a *filler* — just because your curriculum gives it a time slot — or because it sounds spiritual to include it in your studies?

II. Teaching Tools

1. A prepared heart (on your part)
2. God's Word, the Bible
3. A world map
4. A globe
5. Mission books — prepare a lending library and index file system
6. Mission records — several available
7. Mission songs — attractively set up on poster board or use songbooks
8. Pictures of people of the world mounted on large construction paper sheets
9. Large puzzles of children of the world
10. Coloring papers — from mission coloring books
11. "Vocabulary Scroll" — May be prepared on white or yellow shelf paper
12. Curios — things to make children *curious* about other places
13. Samples of handmade gifts that children can make (bookmarks, quilts)
14. Prayer cards
15. Prayer letters
16. Mission board periodicals
17. Flannelgraph stories — mission biographies or Bible stories
18. Flashcard stories — try to stay away from fiction
19. Slide/tape presentations — mission boards have these
20. Sample "mission bulletin boards" — to be duplicated in church homes

III. Specials to Stir Up Interest

1. "Around the World" party — teachers dress in foreign costumes, samples of foreign foods, games, music of other lands, etc.
2. Work Day — bring in materials for each child to make a mission gift.
3. Pen-Pal Day — write as a class, or individually, to missionary children — send picture.
4. Tape Time — class sings and makes a "tape letter" for a missionary.
5. GO YE — take class out to local plaza to hand out tracts.
6. Visit a missionary in a nearby town.

IV. *Which Route to Travel*
  A. **Teaching Strictly Biblical Principles of Missions**
    1. Great Commission — our marching orders — check
       out four Gospels!
       Song: "I Love To Tell The Story"
    2. Submission — "Here am I — send me"
    3. Fields of the World — Acts 1:8
       Song: "Jesus Loves the Little Children" (red/yellow/
       black/white)
       God's all-inclusive love!
       Home Missions — whatever country you were born
       and raised in . . .
           Japanese Boy — Japan
           German Boy — Germany
           Brazilian Girl — Brazil
       Foreign Missions — all other countries (besides your
       home country)
           Japanese Boy — England
           German Boy — America
           Brazilian Girl — Africa

       Illustrate travel distances by using familiar localities.
       For example, in New England a trip to the ocean is
       one hour. Show distances on a map and try to help
       each child understand the concepts of time and
       travel.
    4. Prayer support — 1 Samuel 12:23 and many other
       verses show the importance of prayer. Incorporate
       prayer letters (requests) and prayer cards (remind-
       ers) into this time.
    5. Giving to missions — Philippians 4
       Instruct in monthly support sent out by local church.
       (Use father's/mother's paycheck for example)
  B. **Vocabulary Instruction** — using a vocabulary scroll,
     pinpoint particular words to teach your class.

    1. Day 1   *Great Commission* (Matt. 28)
               Missionary (Paul — "What Wilt Thou Have
               Me To Do?")
               Missions (Acts 1:8)
                   Give out "green" bookmark — "GO"
                   Stick 1 cent (penny) on bookmark —
                   "One Sent"
                   Print mission verses on bookmark

2. Day 2   *Field* (Foreign and Home, Acts 1:8)
3. Day 3   *Deputation* and *Support* (Chart showing missionary's expenses)
4. Day 4   *Prayer Cards* (Use display bulletin board to show your missionaries under support). Relate to how children give out pictures of themselves to grandma, aunts and cousins as a reminder of what they look like.
5. Day 4   *Prayer Letters*. Relate to the children's desire to receive or send newsy letters to Grandma or Aunt Betty, showing how we want to share special news with people we love.

     We should have a special place in our hearts for the missionaries — EVERY LETTER is important. They are sharing their lives with us.
6. Day 5   *Furlough* — Reporting time! Missionaries visit the churches that send *support* money and let the people know what has been done for Christ during the three or four years they were on the *field*.

     Outfit and Passage (O & P) — Plane or boat fare plus all the personal and field supplies they will need for four years. (Can you imagine having to buy four years' supply of *all your* clothes? Four years of toothpaste, soap, even "nibbly" foods?)

C. **Continuous Flash Card Story** (Non-fiction)

1. Choose a story with some depth that relates Bible truths concerning missions. (Some are action-packed thrillers but teach nothing profitable.) Also, check through the story to see if a particular "non-Baptistic" mission is mentioned. Only use reliable publishers and even then — check it out!
2. Be sure to know the story. Be familiar with geographical locations and pronounciation of "unusual" names.
3. Keep eye contact with your pupils. You are not teaching the walls, the ceiling or the floor!
4. Encourage the children to participate in a *short* review of the story before going on to another day's segment.

5. Stimulate, challenge and encourage some self-examination among pupils. Are they saved? Are they ready to follow Christ? Get them to think about their future and service.

D. Missionary Biographies

Much needed because they are not being taught to any age groups. These biographies establish a good background for future teachings in missions.

1. Hudson Taylor
2. Adoniram Judson
3. Count Zindendorf
4. David Brainard
5. Jonathan Goforth

Use maps, flannelgraph figures and pictures of each country and the people. Make these great men come *alive* to the pupils.

Mission update: Relate how missions can be carried on in that country TODAY!

You could wrap up your closing day by allowing some of the more interested pupils to go out on home missions work with one of the teachers. Have a supply of suitable tracts for children.

In Conclusion: A combination of

A *or* B   plus   C *or* D

(10 min.)   (20 min.)

would cover all the bases for introducing missions to your class.

For the juniors and older classes, enlarge upon the chart showing The Steps to Becoming a Missionary, emphasizing the importance of the local church in the life of a missionary.

Steps to becoming a Missionary

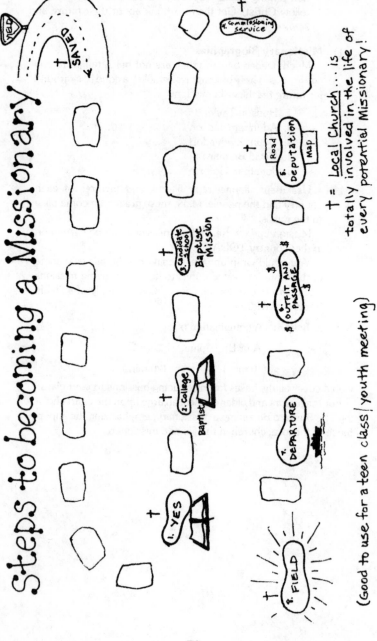

YIELD

SAVED

1. YES

2. College Baptist

3. Candidate School Baptist Mission

4. Commissioning service

5. OUTFIT AND PASSAGE $ $ $

6. Deputation Road Map

7. DEPARTURE

8. FIELD

† = Local Church . . . is totally involved in the life of every potential Missionary!

(Good to use for a teen class / youth meeting)

STUDY
MATERIAL #2

To effectively present this study, it would be wise to research the topic for yourself and see what the Lord would have you to say. It touches on many "ouchy" subjects, yet ones that need to be brought to light.

This material could be presented over several months and possibly allow different women the opportunity to take part. Under "Sharing" you might have the women bring in some of the things mentioned.

> *What? know ye not that your body is the temple of the Holy Ghost which is in you, which ye have of God, and ye are not your own? For ye are bought with a price: therefore glorify God in your body, and in your spirit, which are God's (1 Cor. 6:19, 20).*

SAMPLE

HOW YOUR PERSONAL TESTIMONY
AFFECTS OTHER LADIES

Personal Testimony . . . 1 John 1:1-4
Unable to hold back our enthusiasm — we share the story of our salvation — and the things that the Lord has done

Testimony . . . evidence, proof, solemn declaration, profession

Affect . . . to produce an *effect* — produce a result, purpose, mental impression, realization, consequence

THE SPOTLIGHT IS ON *You* —

ON STAGE . . . ALL THE TIME

What others see, observe, hear

Let's explore some avenues of personal relationships

CHRIST

YOU	Family
YOU	Neighbors
YOU	Co-Workers
	(On the job)
YOU	Old-Time Friends
YOU	Ladies in the
	Church

YOU . . . (Sharing)

Recipes
Menu Suggestions
Kitchen & Laundry Helps
Sewing Hints
Garden Foods
Plant Starts
Craft Ideas
Beauty Tips

Practical Standpoint

YOU . . . (Just plain you!)

Cleanliness
  (personal hygiene)
Neatness
Dress Habits
Hospitality
Your Mouth (What
  goes in —
  What
  comes out)
Behavior in Public

YOU . . . (Qualities Others
  Look For)

Love
Faithfulness
Loyalty
Understanding
Giving
Sacrifice
Kindness
Trust
Patience
Truthfulness
Tolerance
Reliability

Modesty/Humility
Teachableness
Courage
Steadfastness
Enthusiasm
Self-Control
Cheerfulness
Sincerity
Reliance on Christ
Reality of your salvation

STUDY
MATERIAL #3

"SCATTERING PRECIOUS SEED" (Ps. 126:5, 6) is a self-explanatory topic — one we need to explore, but often choose to ignore!

My, how we can totally wrap ourselves up in mission work, but ignore the plea of our own homes, neighborhoods, towns and states. God could use all sorts of miracles, but He desires to use people. He desires to have us combine our **faith** with **works**!

Have you ever noticed how the "yakkiest" people are complete cowards when it comes to visitation? The truth is . . . we're scared! (Deut. 31:8).

Your leader could use the following outline — enlarge upon it as the Lord directs. Encourage interaction — let your people get some of their fears out in the open.

SCATTERING PRECIOUS SEED . . .

I. *Verses to Examine . . .*   1.
                                2.
                                3.

II. *Materials . . .*   1.
                         2.
                         3.

III. *Non-Materials . . .*   1. **Prayer**
                              2. **Power**
                              3. **Purpose**
                              4. **Presence**

IV. *Partcipants . . .*   1. People to **GO**
                           2. People to **Stay**

V. *Purpose*   1. People to visit

VI. *Visitation . . .*   1. Use the situation
                          2. Move quickly to reason

VII. *Extra tips . . .*   1. Appearance
                           2. Notice things
                           3. Your reaction

STUDY
MATERIAL #4

When missionaries make reference to the following words, many people "draw a blank."

Have someone with mission "know how" define each word and give an explanatory example of each one.

A knowledge of these terms will be an asset in understanding and teaching missions. Make personal listings of the many missionary Scripture verses.

Make a neatly printed scroll and display it in one of the teaching classrooms. Keep this information before the people.

GREAT COMMISSION
VISION
BURDEN
CALLED — TO SERVE
SENT — BY GOD
MISSIONARY
CANDIDATE SCHOOL
MISSION AGENCY (BOARD)
FIELD — HOME
FIELD — FOREIGN
DEPUTATION
SUPPORT
OUTFIT

PASSAGE
COMMISSIONED
VETERAN
APPOINTEE
DEPARTURE
PRAYER CARD
PRAYER LETTER
PRAYER WARRIOR
NATIONAL
CURIOS
FURLOUGH
INDIGENOUS
HARVEST

STUDY MATERIAL #5

"Furlough, My Foot!"
Miss Agnes Haik
A.B.W.E. Natal, Brazil

Facts & Figures

5½ weeks/38 days — New England Itinerary

Spoke in 11 churches: 2 Conferences (4 days each)
4 Sundays
4 Prayer Meetings
1 Baby Shower
3 Ladies' Fellowships
2 Christian Schools
1 Youth Meeting
1 Fellowship Social

24 days

                    3 Visiting Churches
                    6 Traveling Days
                  __1 Ladies' Social
                   34 days

                    4 days to fit in 7 dinner engagements,
                        to write 10 letters, plus 1 prayer
                        letter
                    "Shopping" every extra moment
                        for her return to the field

WITH DEPARTURE DATE SET FOR THANKSGIVING
DAY (After many frenzied phone calls for final confirmation
on flights) . . . What does our missionary do with her final
two weeks at home? (Rest and drink Coke? *No-o-o-o-o!*)

1. Requests from Brazil for —
            microwave shelf — just the right size
            toaster oven element
            drafting tools — just what Aggie knows all about!
            yard goods
            special cologne — a brand she never heard of!
2. Shopping for 3½ years' worth of personal supplies
3. Shopping for 3 Christmas seasons
4. Shopping for baby gifts
5. New Prayer Cards
6. Medical exam
7. Passport
8. Travel agent/finalize departure
9. Insurance forms/final details to be checked
10. Mission up-date
11. Packing barrels
12. Sending packages ahead
13. Mailing thank-you's
14. Finalize budget/accounts/bills
15. Farewell — New Jersey church
16. Farewell — with family on Thanksgiving . . . off to
        airport!

(Is it any wonder that Aggie's letters sometimes look like
frazzled nerve ends!)

As you review Agnes Haik's fall schedule in New England, it might cause you to think upon the missions program in your church.

This is also a reminder of the time Aggie spent with YOU — and to remind you to *pray* for *her*. Many times our missionaries are a "hit or miss" affair when it comes to our church prayer life.

You undoubtedly have received her December prayer letter, which was hastily written in order that you might know that, indeed, she is back at work! (As if she *ever* stopped.)

Aggie is always very careful to present the VICTORY side of her work in Brazil — she is not the type of missionary to play on our sympathy. Therefore, I am taking the liberty to share some personal prayer requests for her and to tell of the pluses and minuses of deputation.

PRAYER REQUESTS

1. Ants, roaches, rats, etc.
2. Automobile — cost of upkeep, gasoline
3. Apartment — monthly rent, furnishings
4. Health
5. Eating habits — she needs discipline — she does not eat properly
6. Re-adjustment to culture
7. Unpacking
8. "Laughter" — there is little to laugh about, so she doesn't
9. Responsibilities and decisions that fall on the single woman
10. The "indecencies" she is exposed to
11. Rest (physical and spiritual) — her work is twenty-four hours a day

DEPUTATION

"PLUS"

1. Warm "open doors" in churches
2. Meeting new pastors
3. Making new friends
4. People who prepared favorite foods

"MINUS"

1. Last minute cancellation and dropping of support (all of particular church's missionaries were dropped — pastor said they couldn't afford to have missionaries

5. Thoughtful gestures like warm fireside visits to relax and warm her weary bones

6. Folks who went out of their way to allow her the time to visit former friends from way back when

7. Men who allowed her to help with a men's prayer breakfast and taught her how to flip pancakes without a spatula (eggs, too)

8. Individuals who gave special personal gifts: a lovely quilt made to order, musical items needed for the field, the young mother who whipped up several dresses while caring for her four children

9. The young woman who so graciously offered to set up and print new prayer cards

10. Pastors who were alert to the need of "interviewing" visiting missionaries

11. Churches where people so generously prepared for Aggie's visit, sewing and working months ahead of time

12. The surprise birthday wishes and the birthday party where new and old friends showered Aggie with gifts (Ahem — *Nov. 1*)

under support).

2. Not giving a missionary a chance to get her breath after a l-o-n-g drive from previous engagement.

3. Scheduling "early morning to late evening" meetings without a personal break. We forget sometimes that missionaries need to do some "soakin' " as well as "spillin'. "

4. Singing "only" mission songs — they would love to hear some of the hymns we enjoy each week. (*They* don't hear hymns on the field and *we* need the challenge of mission songs to fill the gap between missionary visits.)

5. Not considering *travel expenses* — this should be given to every speaker *over* and *above* the love offering. Speakers many times use all their offerings to travel back and forth to 2 or 3 meetings daily plus for meals. Also, to check out the condition of the car. Loosen up with the "green" to spring for a tune-up.

PART 5

The Ladies' Missionary Fellowship

9
The ladies' missionary fellowship

For we are labourers together with God . . . (1 Cor. 3:9a).

The Ladies' Missionary Fellowship is an auxiliary organization working in accordance with your church constitution under the watchful eye of your pastor and executive board.

PURPOSES:

1. To promote interest in missions within the local church and wherever the sphere of Christian influence extends.

2. To assist the missionaries by providing for both personal and field needs.

3. To assist the church missions committee in promoting the Annual Missionary Conference.

MEMBERSHIP: The membership shall consist of Christian women active in the fellowship of your church.

OFFICERS: (Qualifications)

1. **President** —Must have a zealous heart for missions
Must have leadership ability
Must have organizational ability

2. **Vice-President**	—Same as president
3. **Secretary/ Treasurer**	—Must know the job Must have an interest in typing, keeping books, corresponding, etc. and sharing the burden for missions
4. **Projects Chairman**	—Must be qualified to handle all situations— all types of projects (sewing, art, etc.) and capable of directing Must be able to plan a "good" missionary cupboard

All officers must be members of the church in good standing and faithful to all services of the church.

SUCCESSFUL MEETINGS

A) **Do** keep them simple . . .
B) **Do** keep projects moving . . .
C) **Do** include work, prayer, short devotional . . .
D) **Do not** lag into gossip sessions . . .
E) **Do not** use them as an excuse for social wing-dings . . .
F) **Do not** be wasteful with God's money . . .

*Are you ready? Remember: missions is not a private affair concerning a few interested individuals . . . your **church** is missions!*

Suggestion: Have your Ladies' Missionary Fellowship meeting on the First Tuesday of the month.

EVERY WOMAN MAY BE INCLUDED

DRIVERS	DEVOTIONS	DESSERT	PRAYER
for pick-up — PHONECALLS to invite Ladies to attend.	10 Min. — Rotate among the Ladies	Prepare coffee & tea at the lunch-dessert — (Rotate among the Ladies.)	Read Prayer Letters — Take part in a prayer circle.

PREPARE A MONTHLY "DUTY LIST" FOR A YEAR

Recommended Schedule:

9:30 A.M. to 9:50 A.M.	DEVOTIONS AND PRAYER CIRCLE
9:50 A.M. to 12:00 Noon	WORK
12:00 Noon to 12:15 P.M.	LUNCH
12:15 P.M. to 12:30 P.M.	OFFERING STUDY/BUSINESS
12:30 P.M. to 2:15 P.M.	WORK
2:15 P.M. to 2:30 P.M.	CLEAN-UP

QUARTERLY EVENING MEETINGS

1. February — Study Program, Business, Present the year's program, Prayer, Refreshments
2. May — Mother-Daughter Banquet—Guest Speaker
3. August — "Kick-Off" Pot Luck Supper—Extensive study in missions, Programs, Slides, etc.
4. December — Christmas Tea—Invite Jr./Sr. High girls and another ladies' group. Guest Speaker

OCCASIONAL DAY SPECIALS

1. Instead of the usual sandwiches for lunch, plan to have a "Salad Bowl Buffet." Each lady can prepare a favorite salad and bring it to the meeting.

2. In the winter the ladies can pitch in for the cost of a nice fish chowder, homemade soup or beef stew with hot bread.

3. At the December meeting have ladies bring in their favorite Christmas recipes (cookies, fruit cakes, nut breads, etc.) all made up and gift wrapped as a special treat for your pastor's wife (to ease the burden of Christmas entertaining).

MISSIONARY CUPBOARD

SUGGESTED POINT SYSTEM

A $	.10	item equals	1 point
A $	1.00	item equals	10 points
A	$10.00	item equals	100 points

Determine the amount of points for each guest speaker:

A one-night guest may receive 150 points
A week-end guest may receive 200 points
A conference guest may receive 300 points

* * * * * * * * * * * * * * * * *

PROJECTS

Tupperware—have one party a year—for general cupboard or a special missionary

Pillow Cases—make one from border prints—1⅛ yard each

Instant Quilts—5 yards of print for top (2½ and 2½ join with center seam)

5 yards solid color or full flat sheet for backing

1 used—clean—sheet blanket (polyester fill)

Place filler smoothly on wrong side of print fabric—tack edges

Pin solid backing to right side of print fabric—three layers—stitch around three edges (leave lower edge open)

Turn "right side out"—*smooth*—slip-stitch bottom edge

Tie "knots" with bright color yarn every 6 or 8 inches—trim as desired. (Good idea to *finish stitch* two rows around entire quilt.)

It is like making a jumbo pillow case and it takes a lot of patience!

Aprons—make half aprons, cobblers, children's cover-ups

Ties—men really appreciate these. They are inexpensive to make.

Bandages—3″, 4″, 5″—from used sheets

Favors—good for missionaries to use as "awards." Save bathroom tissue rolls—cut in half—insert small gift inside each roll—cover with crepe paper—tie with yarn—put a pretty sticker on seam

Bookmarks—make from felt and decorate. They make good prizes.

Pot Holders and Placemats—Make from scrap materials

Visualized Stories—may be purchased from Baptist Mid-Missions—painted or colored—then backed

Patchwork Quilts—make from scraps

Visuals—collect money for the purchase of the entire series of *Footsteps of Faith* from the Bible Club Movement. These along with the lesson book are excellent for your cupboard. Have the visuals cut out by ladies.

Eyeglass Pins—old lenses, cute little pictures, pin backings (inexpensive)

Socks, Hats, Booties

Slippers, Scarves—good for those who knit or crochet

Stuffed Animals—many patterns available

Wordless Books—from construction paper

Craft Gifts—spice ropes, decorated bamboo mats and brooms, wreaths, etc.

Clothing—baby layettes, children's p.j.'s, robes—very good for the missionary children

Food Showers—good for home missionaries or missionaries home on furlough

*   *

. . . **Don't** neglect the ladies unable to attend meetings—see that you have a good supply of "homework" available.

Emphasize **neatness** . . . this may have to be done at every meeting.

And whatsoever ye do in word or deed, do all in the name of the Lord Jesus, giving thanks to God and the Father by him (Col. 3:17).

* *

VISUALIZED STORIES: Baptist Mid-Missions
4205 Chester Ave.
Cleveland, Ohio 44103

VISUALS: Bible Club Movement, Inc.
237 Fairfield Ave.
Upper Darby, PA 19082

Bible Visuals
Box 93
Landisville, PA 17538

YEARLY SERVICE QUESTIONNAIRE

This questionnaire is of great value in determining the talents available in your ladies' group. It can also be a time-saver—you won't have to run around trying to locate willing workers at the last minute. It gives the ladies an opportunity to function in the areas where they are most comfortable.

SAMPLE

LADIES' MISSIONARY FELLOWSHIP   YEAR _____

Name ....
Address ....
Mailing Address ....
Phone ....
Birthday ....
Anniversary ....
Favorite Color ....
Hobbies ....

Yes, for the Lord and with His help, I would be willing to do the following for missions:

1. Knit
2. Crochet
3. Sew
4. Embroidery
5. Liquid embroidery
6. Cut out patterns
7. Paper work—cut out visuals
8. Roll bandages
9. Quilts: squares _____ tie _____
10. Crafts
11. Grow plants
12. Flannelgraph scenes
13. Lettering & printing
14. Paint
15. Type
16. Create novel invitations
17. Color & back visuals

1. Set up tables
2. Serve tables
3. "Attend" buffet table
4. Be a greeter
5. Phone call invitations
6. Usher
7. Pray
8. Games
9. Work on decorating
10. Correspondence
11. Make & give out invitations
12. Sing: solo _____ group _____
13. Lead singing
14. Lead prayer time
15. Lead short devotional
16. Mission research & presentation
17. Read biography & report

1. I would like to invite another group here for a special meeting. Yes _____ No _____

2. I would like to have the Ladies' Missionary Fellowship sponsor an Adult Fellowship Mission Night. Yes _____ No _____

. . . Serve him with a perfect heart and with a willing mind . . . (1 Chron. 28:9).

10
The constitution:

LMF Constitution Ave. Free Spirit Blvd. — A Fork In The Road . . .

Which route to follow? A formal constitution or an informal, unwritten code? After much personal thought and deliberation, I have decided to include both routes. Having travelled both of these roads, I can honestly say that there are advantages and disadvantages to both.

This book has been prepared primarily as a handbook to assist laymen in establishing sound, but practical, mission programming in the local church. Your pastor's own personal convictions plus the voice of the people will be the determining factor as to the depth of organization to be established in your church. This book does not pacify or embrace any particular group of churches or pastors, nor does it aim to offend any fundamental Baptist fellowships.

Being well aware of the fact that there will be association churches, strictly independent churches, and isolated independent churches having access to this material, I know that there will be some ideas accepted or rejected because of the individual stand of these various churches and pastors. This is fully understandable. Actually, this ability to choose or reject an idea acclaims the autonomous stance of the local church and is very Biblical!

Because of previous "convention" problems tied in with militant leadership, many pastors fear delving into anything beyond pastor-deacon leadership. Reaching past this point to include a formalized organization among the ladies would cause some pastors to revolt. These churches should choose a simplified program for the ladies. For example, instead of a formal Ladies' Missionary Fellowship, the pastor could coordinate a missions program for the ladies with the help of one key individual. The pastor should choose a woman who has a true vision for missions and meets the "qualifications" listed for officers.

In reality, this woman would unofficially be acting in the role of missions chairman for the Ladies' Missionary Fellowship. The only difference would be that she would coordinate the missions programs and work with the pastor.

In many cases, this one-on-one basis could lead to a more relaxed situation. There would not be the million-and-one suggestions, complaints, and discussions which occasionally taint the missions committee meetings. It must also be stated that this key woman should have the confidence and the support of both the pastor and the ladies.

On the other hand, for those pastors who are comfortable with a formal Ladies' Missionary Fellowship, it has been very beneficial for the ladies to operate within the confines of a formal constitution. The guidelines for duties are clearly defined—they have received the approval and blessing of the pastor and church to function in this manner. Many times a constitution saves a lot of embarrassment if points of controversy arise. It also assures the church that there is no detraction from church standards.

Some will turn the page, see the word **constitution**, and say "No way!" Others will say, "Just what we need!"

Would "to each his own" be a good rebuttal? Not really! Search your hearts and use much prayer and wisdom to seek out God's plan for your church.

CONSTITUTION

Not all groups care to work within the confines of a formal constitution. The reason is that constitutions are seldom followed. It would be well to pray and seriously consider the value of a constitution. If you decide to go this route, then be faithful to abide by the guidelines which will be adopted by your Ladies' Missionary Fellowship.

SAMPLE

ARTICLE I: NAME

The name of this group shall be known as the **Ladies' Missionary Fellowship** (or Circle) of the _____ Baptist Church.

ARTICLE II: PURPOSE

The Purposes are:
1. To promote interest in missions within the local church and wherever the sphere of Christian influence extends.
2. To further the spread of the gospel at home and abroad.
3. To help provide for missionaries' personal needs and needs within their mission fields.
4. To assist the missions committee in executing the Annual Missions Conference.

ARTICLE III: MEMBERSHIP

The membership of this group shall consist of Christian women in the fellowship of the _____ Baptist Church.

ARTICLE IV: OFFICERS AND CHAIRMEN

Officers and chairmen of this organization must be active members in good standing of the _____ Baptist Church.

Section 1. **Officers**—the officers of this group shall be:
President
Vice-President/Secretary
Treasurer

Section 2. **Elections**

The officers of this organization shall be elected annually, holding office from January 1 until December 31. Nominations of the nominating committee shall be posted two weeks before the election, which will take place during the December meeting. Nominations must meet the approval of the church Executive Board, and the acceptance of the persons being nominated.

As soon as possible after the election, the President shall call a meeting of the officers to prayerfully discuss the requirements of each committee and the potentialities within the membership. Guided by the Holy Spirit and the counsel of the other officers, the President shall, with the consent of the appointees, make the appointments of chairmen and announce them in the following meeting. These appointments shall be:
Projects Chairman (Work Chairman)
Social Chairman

In case of limited membership, the officers may assume the duties of the chairman. The officers shall constitute the **Executive Committee**—they may or may not extend this committee to include the chairman.

Section 3. **Term of Office**

Officers and chairmen shall serve for one year. It is recommended that no officer or chairman be nominated to serve for more than four consecutive years unless there are no available replacements.

ARTICLE V: MEETINGS

This organization shall meet regularly on the first Tuesday of the month or subject to change at call of the Executive Committee. The Work Day and the Program Study shall be combined until the group can handle two meetings a month.

Article VI: Amendments

This constitution may be amended at any regular meeting of the organization by a two-thirds vote of the members following the recommendation of the Executive Committee. Amendments must be reviewed by the pastor and deacons and announced prior to the meeting.

By-Laws

Article I: Duties of Officers

Section 1. **President**

The president shall preside at all Ladies' Missionary Fellowship meetings, programs and Executive Committee meetings. The President shall oversee all activities and programs of the Ladies' Missionary Fellowship.

The president shall be responsible for the instruction and leadership of the Ladies' Missionary Fellowship in mission knowledge, mission Bible study and prayer.

The president is responsible for the successful functioning of offices and committees. She shall keep records for the year showing the overall successes and shortcomings. The information can be used to determine ways and means of developing the goals and objectives of the Ladies' Missionary Fellowship.

Section 2. **Vice-President/Secretary**

The Vice-president shall serve in cooperation with the President and shall perform all duties of that office in the absence of the president. The vice-president shall also perform the duties of secretary, which is to record the minutes of the organization and of the Executive Committee. It shall also be the duty of the secretary to prepare correspondence as directed.

In the absence of the secretary an "acting secretary" may be assigned for the day, turning all reports over to the elected secretary as soon as possible. All records are the property of the Ladies' Missionary Fellowship (the church) and are to be turned in as part of the church files at the close of each year.

Section 3. **Treasurer**

The treasurer shall have general oversight of the finances of the organization. The treasurer shall be responsible for the receipt, deposit, and disbursement of all funds upon order of the organization or Executive Committee. The treasurer shall present a financial report at all meetings of the organization, also at meetings of the Executive Committee.

All financial records are the property of the church and need to be turned in as part of the church files at the close of the year.

Section 1. Special committees shall be appointed by the president or by the Executive Committee as needs arise.

a. **Nominating Committee** of three members shall be appointed by the Executive Committee in September. This committee shall present a list of nominees for officers of the organization at the annual election.

b. **Social Chairman** is responsible for the luncheons at the Ladies' Missionary Fellowship Work Days and to prepare a chart for each month (for a year) listing the ladies who will bring in dessert for each month. The Social Chairman will see that lunch time preparations are ready on time, provide necessary supplies and supervise "clean up." Also, for any special night meetings or banquets under the direction of the Executive Committee, the Social Chairman will supervise the assigned committee workers and plan and execute the social.

c. **Work Chairman** shall be responsible for purchasing the materials, setting out the "work day" materials at each meeting, directing the project making at each meeting, and directing the clean-up after each meeting.

The Work Chairman (also known as Projects Chairman) is to keep the missionary cupboard in order and keep inventory of supplies and gifts that were made or given out.

The Work Chairman is advised as to work projects under the direction of the Executive Committee and is responsible to give a report at each Executive Committee meeting.

ARTICLE III: STANDING RULES

1. Members elected or appointed to fill a vacancy of an unexpired term for more than seven months shall be considered to have served a full term, but shall not be ineligible for the full term of any office in the succeeding election.

2. Officers and chairmen may select one or more assistants from the membership to implement their work. To be eligible to serve in this capacity one must have attended at least six meetings within a twelve month period.

3. An officer being absent from the regular meetings for three consecutive months shall be automatically removed from that position.

11
Pitfalls of the ladies' missionary fellowship

You have just completed several pages of "how to" organize a Ladies' Missionary Fellowship in your church. This *can* be one of the most productive areas of church ministries for the ladies. It involves *all* the ladies! It leaves little room for competitive jealousy or flaring tempers if it functions under the banner of **love.** (Maybe the theme song for every group should be "His Banner Over Us Is Love.")

Because ladies tend to "clique-up," be "kaffee-klatschers," become "phone-mongers" and be a little snippy or tempermental, it is very important to have strong leadership in your group. A compromising, easy-going, always smiling person may function well as a buffer at a social, but not always as an officer of your ladies' group. This type of person will be overwhelmed by all the suggestions and ideas planted in her head by every well-meaning sister in the church. If she forgets the goals set down by the group in order to start pacifying everyone, the fellowship will end in chaos!

Almost every ladies' group has shared some of the following problems at one time or another. Read them over and consider them as "an ounce of prevention that is worth a pound of cure."

1. Once your group is organized and officers are elected (hopefully as a result of prayer, not by the buddy system)—

be sure the **officers meet once a month.** They need to review and prepare for every meeting and they need to band together for mutual support.

Some will say that this isn't necessary—"after all, we're just meeting to sew a little bit—why all the formality?" It is necessary! Any well run business will conduct management meetings!

2. If, per chance, someone is elected as an officer who does not follow the church's policies in missions, do not allow an "over-throw" to take place. Be firm! (Do not permit hours of bantering at an officer's meeting.)

3. You may find a "cold wall" before you one day as you conduct devotions, study, or prayer time. If so, nip it in the bud! (This usually means some ladies have been playing the game of "roast president" at their daily coffee rounds or their convenient "good samaritan" home calls.)

4. One officer may try to usurp another officer's position.

5. Don't "create" positions to accommodate an individual. Allow that person to work alongside the others until next year's election. This magnificent ball of energy may fizzle out when it gets down to the nitty-gritty of actual "work"! Sometimes you need that time as a proving ground.

6. Sometimes ladies will show up at a meeting with materials and work which has not been approved, intending to do their own thing!

Very diplomatically thank them, remove the work materials, and continue with the work which has been planned for the day. A rough thing to do but it must be done!

7. Eliminate all gossip from your meetings! You cannot allow the ladies to get caught up in this.

Be especially careful when visitors attend your meetings. It will not only discourage a newcomer to hear how you manipulated a person at last week's visitation but she may also doubt the sincerity of your endeavors of friendship toward her!

8. Be sure to have all work supplies ready *before* the meeting. It should all be laid out neatly on tables for the ladies to choose their work for the day. (A posted worksheet is

beneficial.) If the ladies have to stand around waiting for things to be hauled out and hashed over, they will probably stay home next month.

9. The Ladies' Missionary Fellowship is an auxiliary branch of the missions committee—in retrospect, its meetings are the same as any other church meeting or service. Therefore, proper wearing apparel should be donned by every woman attending the meetings, work days or special programs! A president should not have to request that dresses, nylons or clean hair be the attire for the day. Slacks, jeans, pantsuits, braless sundresses and bare legs are out of order!

The nicer you look the better you feel, and the meetings will be evidence of this.

10. TRUE SAYINGS. These legitimate and illegitimate complaints have come from ladies who claim:

. . . It took two years to make one quilt!

. . . My ideas are never heard!

. . . Missions isn't a "ten minute devotion" and a "twenty minute donut dunk"!

. . . I sat through an entire day and no one spoke to me!

. . . All the other women get together outside of church, and they forget the fact that I exist!

. . . We never finish anything!

. . . If we aren't going to work, I'm going to stay home!

. . . Why can't we dress up our meetings—they are so drab!

. . . The work chairman always shows up late!

. . . We never pray!

. . . Don't ask me to pray!

. . . I'll come only if I can bring my radio to hear Brother _____ at 10:15! (A tear slipping down the cheek.)

. . . It's all older women who know everything, but never want to show us how!

. . . All the young mothers stick together and forget an old body doesn't mean an old heart! Well, we like fun too!

. . . She'll hold that office forever!

. . . No one will accept an office—they're afraid of work!

. . . My family comes first—and I wash on Tuesdays . . .

don't look for me at your meeting!

. . . We never discuss any business, and no one knows what's going on!

. . . Business meetings are too long—we don't need to know everything—that's what officers are for!

. . . I'm on a diet! Why do we have to have dessert?

. . . A second meeting this month!!! W-h-h-hy??? (High-pitched whine.)

. . . Why do we have to have day meetings—my friend, so and so, has to work and can't attend!

. . . No meetings at night for me! My husband wouldn't be caught dead eating a *casserole* while I went to a ladies' meeting!

. . . Yes, saved ten years—but, please don't ask me for a testimony!

. . . You're such a good leader, you give the book report— I feel so inadequate!

11. Finally, a note about the PASTOR'S WIFE. This lady can "make" or "break" a ladies' fellowship.

She may be:

. . . Apathetic! Never shows her face at a missionary meeting. (And never even inquires about the meetings.)

. . . Non-committal! Just smiles (with mouth, not eyes) and never makes any positive comments—leaving everyone in a quandary. Does she approve or not??!!

. . . Overbearing! Uses her position to overpower the group and belittles suggestions coming from the "lesser" folks.

Also, uses her Bible knowledge to discourage and defeat women trying their first steps at devotionals or prayer.

. . . Jealous! Pouts, making the other women give in to her every whim while the women hold back their opinions for fear of offending the pastor's wife.

She may be:

. . . Supportive! Shows up for the meetings. Smiling— ready to work alongside all the women. (She may not always be able to stay all day due to other positional commitments.)

. . . Encouraging! Especially to the officers. Lets the ladies know that she approves of what is going on, and displays love and warmth to the officers. (This will encourage others to accept an office in the future.)

. . . Cooperative! Asks how she may help. Willing to sit in on officers' meetings in an ex officio capacity, if asked, and not offended if not asked.

. . . Watchful! Carefully observes the reactions of the women, and sensitive to any trouble spots. Then in a loving way, informs the officers of areas which could stand improvement (without crushing them to a pulp).

. . . Hospitable! Has the open-door policy with the ladies (providing they do not abuse it). Occasionally invites the group to hold a meeting in her home.

. . . Available! Pastors' wives have many irons in the fire, so cannot put all their efforts into one special program of the church. It is a wise pastor's wife who is willing to go shopping with the project's chairman (just to be that needed warm body), go out to lunch now and then with the group's president, attend a special conference with the ladies, offer to take part in a program, and especially to be that much-needed prayer warrior!

. . . Confidante! Should some personal situations arise among the ladies, she must learn to keep a confidence. These things may be discussed with her husband, the pastor, beyond earshot of their children, no matter what their ages! (Out of the mouths of the preacher's children slips many a morsel of gossip from "roast the congregation" sessions at dinnertime!)

[A Note For the Men: Men, pray for the ladies in your church, offer your services, give praise and encouragement and be willing to take over at home occasionally so your wife may have a chance to attend these meetings. Be supportive and be willing to admit that you run into some of the same pitfalls at your meetings, too.]

All the "sticky" things which you have just read were not written for you to get "smug" about and start placing your church ladies into each situation. They were written

111

as *true happenings* to help *you* have a super ladies fellowship. Clear up any faulty areas which might hinder the work of missions in your church.

PART 6

Programs

12
Programs:
perils and pleasures

*That which we have seen and heard declare we unto you,
that ye also may have fellowship with us: and truly our
fellowship is with the Father, and with his Son Jesus Christ.*
(1 John 1:3)

We will now enter a very controversial area of missions. Unless you are fortunate enough to be part of a truly loving, flexible group of believers, this could be perilous ground.

There must be a very definite line drawn between church missions and church socials. Otherwise, the social committee may assume it is to organize a particular social and may be highly offended when they realize that the missions committee has already taken care of the details!

Ground rules need to be laid down—and followed! Your pastor and Executive Board should oversee the decisions. A suggestion is that "if the social involves a missionary speaker or has a mission emphasis, let the Ladies' Missionary Fellowship draw up the plans." Set guidelines for your church social committee—such as "the social committee shall have charge of the all-church fellowships that are not specifically under the direction of the missions committee, Sunday School department, adult fellowship, or youth group."

Now that we have removed the first obstacle, let's briefly move on to several more.

I. The world's word is *casual* . . .
   The church's word is *orderly* . . .

Anyone can throw food on the table any-which-way, with mix-'n-match everything, and come up with a half-baked mess. We call it "casual"!

Why, oh why, do we treat the Lord's work this way?

Any social program of the church should be organized as thoroughly as any other avenue of service for the Lord. PRAY-ORGANIZE-ASSIGN-EXECUTE as unto the Lord. Neatness and cleanliness should be two important factors in preparing food for a social function—along with palatability (it should taste good).

The eyes of the world are upon us when we prepare for these affairs, so we must watch our testimony! Not only should everything we prepare be well organized and attractive, but we should be the same.

II. *Our children*—bless their little hearts! I sincerely mean this, because the parents are the ones who need the spanking when it comes to obnoxious Janey or Johnny.

Parents are the foremost offenders when it comes to breaking rules to suit their own petty idiosyncrasies! Many a delightful social has been turned into a disaster because of children (parents). Some parents claim they cannot (or will not) be separated from their children to attend an adult social. Funny thing—the children go to school without mom or dad; dad goes to work without mom and the children; mom and dad get babysitters for other affairs (like the shop or office Christmas party); on and on!

A well-balanced all-year church calendar should include regular programs for the several age brackets plus several all-church socials. Sneaking your child into an adult social, hiding your child somewhere in the church or private home, pleading for your child to be the "exception," using your position of leadership to by-pass rules, teaches your child to be dishonest and rebellious. It also causes resentment among other parents who were careful to line up a babysitter for their children.

If the social does include children, let's teach our children some manners, Mom and Dad! Nothing can ruin a social more than the children with runny noses (unwiped), dirty hands, messy pants, or coughing over the table, snorting, hacking, grabbing at others, chewing open-mouthed, pushing in line, screaming, demanding seconds, gagging on unfamiliar food, whining, and being a little stinker in general! To save yourself the embarrassment in public—please, oh please, train your child at home! Someday your child will thank you for the time you spent teaching him or her the social graces of life.

III. *Additional training that will pay off. . . .*

Include your men and teens. A lot of extra trouble, you say, because, after all, women can do it more easily. This may be true, but our teens and men need to participate occasionally in the planning and in the preparation of socials. We, as ladies, need to be patient and willing to take the time to teach them. There are many fine chefs in our churches just waiting to be used, many young men fully capable of serving as waiters and young women wanting to learn the proper methods of hostessing.

Many young mothers plead for "casual" simply because they have never been taught social proprieties and etiquette.

IV. *Practical rules to make church entertaining a pleasure*

1. Assign a coordinator (someone with leadership ability).
2. Seek out a good working committee—people who are willing to give of their time and talents.
3. Have cooks, waiters, hosts, hostesses, greeter and a cleanup crew.
4. Promotion: use posters, bulletin notices, newspapers, flyers, personal invitations, radio, and most important of all, the pastor.
5. Have a sign-up list (helps with numbers when planning for food).

6. Use name tags (if many visitors are expected).
7. Have a photographer (keep a church photo album).
8. Records: keep an accurate account of foodstuff, amounts and expenses. (This will make future planning much easier.)
9. Kitchen worksheets: post for each social to eliminate an over-lapping of duties.
10. Kitchen cleanliness—cleanliness—cleanliness
    a. Keep the church kitchen and everything in it spotlessly clean.
    b. All kitchen workers must be free from communicable diseases.
    c. Wash hands!
    d. Keep hair in place, and keep hands out of it.
    e. Hands—finger lickin' good may be okay at home but not in public.
    f. Catch the church mouse—it may be cute, but it is a germ carrier.
    g. Wear aprons!
11. Have all needed equipment and supplies in the church kitchen on the *day before* the social to eliminate jangled nerves. Keep your kitchen well stocked!
12. Have high chairs and booster seats available.
13. Exercise manners—be sure your special guests are served first, along with your pastor and his wife.
14. Meet after each social (coordinator and pastor, or as a committee) to iron out any problem areas.

V. *Social Questionnaire*

On page 120 you will find a sample questionnaire to help all committees of the church make plans "to please the people." You may want to use it as it is or modify it to make it more applicable to your particular church. It is very helpful, and should be given out annually.

Following the questionnaire, you will find twelve programs which hopefully will give you some ideas for your mission socials. Many of these programs have come from my files and have been used successfully to promote missions.

Note: Anyone, I mean **anyone,** can draw up similar programs—if you are willing to take the needed time—if you are socially inclined—if you love people—if you like food—but especially, if you are desirous to see MISSIONS go forward in your church.

SOCIAL INFORMATION QUESTIONNAIRE

NAME _____ ADDRESS _____

In order to plan adult socials which will be to your liking, please check the following:

Yes, I WOULD LIKE TO HELP BY. . .

1. Offering the use of my yard _____
2. Opening my home for a fellowship _____
3. Supplying sports equipment _____
4. Providing transportation _____
5. Extending invitations _____
6. Cooking _____ indoor_____ outdoor _____
7. Setting up _____
8. Cleaning up _____
9. Being a greeter _____
10. Making reservations _____
11. Directing games _____ indoor_____ outdoor _____
12. Leading devotional (men only) _____
13. Working on a food committee _____
14. Opening my home/yard for teen social _____

How often would you like to have an Adult Fellowship?

Once a month _____ Every other month _____ plus "Seasonal Specials" _____

* * * * * * * * * * * * * *

Yes, I WOULD LIKE TO PARTICIPATE IN THE FOLLOWING (OR AM WILLING TO TRY). . . .

	Sports		Yard Games
_____	Bowling	_____	Volleyball
_____	Fishing	_____	Softball
_____	Deep-sea fishing	_____	Archery

_____ Hiking
_____ Roller skating

_____ Horseshoes

Winter Sports

_____ Skiing
_____ Skating
_____ Sledding
_____ Snowmobile

All-Day Church

_____ Visitation
_____ Canvassing
_____ Yard work
_____ Cleaning

*   *   *   *   *   *   *   *   *   *   *   *   *

AWAY TRIPS . . .

_____ Mountains
_____ Ocean
_____ Professional sports
     event
_____ State park family
     outing (B.B.Q.)
_____ Bible camp

_____ Ladies'/Men's
     retreat
_____ Couples' retreat
_____ Visit a fellowship
     sister church
_____ Invite a sister
     church here
_____ Large city

Yes, I WOULD LIKE THE FOLLOWING . . .

_____ Missionary
     speakers
_____ Dinner at a restau-
     rant
_____ Easter Breakfast
_____ Christmas Party
_____ Special films
_____ Destination un-
     known? (Mystery
     trip)

_____ Singspiration
_____ "Baby Picture"
     Who's Who
_____ Yankee Swap Gift
     Exchange
_____ Fall "Harvest Ban-
     quet" (Missions)
_____ Progressive Dinner
_____ Missions Work
     Night

*   *   *   *   *   *   *   *   *   *   *   *   *

Specials AND FOODS I WILL EAT
(OR AM WILLING TO TRY) . . .

_____ "Steak Out"

    _____ Winter

    _____ Summer

_____ Ice-Cream Social

_____ Pizza Party

_____ Fish Fry (Men)

_____ Roast Beef

_____ Polynesian/Chinese

_____ Irish Night

    _____ Boiled Dinner

    _____ Corned Beef

_____ Old Fashioned Box Lunch (Chicken)

_____ Down South Party

_____ Submarine Party

_____ Chowders

    _____ Corn

    _____ Fish

_____ Hawaiian Luau

_____ Mexican Night

_____ Smorgasbord

    _____ European

    _____ Swedish

    _____ French

    _____ German

    _____ Dutch

SAMPLE

PROGRAM #1

Family Watchnight Fellowship

There is no better way to spend New Year's Eve than with your Christian family. This should be a well-organized, but comfortable, evening for all the family. New Year's Eve comes right on the heels of a very busy Christmas season; so, to avoid a lot of hectic, last minute preparations, get everything lined up by the end of November. _Impossible,_ you say? No, _imperative!_

I. _In November_

Get these things out of the way:

1. Purchase all your paper goods.
2. Plan your menu.
3. Make any necessary decorations, posters, invitations.
4. Confirm the date with your guest speaker.
5. Bake and freeze the foods that will keep well.

II. *Theme—Jewish Missions*
1. Contact a missionary who has the reputation of working well among Jewish people—a missionary who is capable of executing a program to include lecture and discussion.
2. There is an excellent film, *The Passover,* which could be part of the evening's program. This film would probably hold the attention of the people better than a slide presentation. Another film, *Dry Bones,* would also fit in well.
3. Be sure to ask your missionary to bring along study material, which could be used at a later date by different age groups.
4. Ask for good promotional materials plus a photograph of the missionary.

III. *Decorations*
1. Locate a large flag with the Star of David and hang it as a back-drop behind your buffet table.
2. Use blue and gold for your decor—possibly blue tablecloths, gold plates and cups, Star of David napkins, candles and accent floral decorations.
3. Have a culture center set up to display the many Jewish pieces you will borrow from the people. It would be well to ask one individual to locate the maps, relics, curios; another individual to study and prepare to answer questions about the pieces (someone who enjoys digging at the library); and an artistic individual to assume the responsibility of setting up an attractive display. All three could "man the table" during the evening.

IV. *Program*

8:00 P.M.— 8:45 P.M.	Workshop . . . "Witnessing to the Jew"
	Lecture and Discussion
8:45 P.M.— 9:15 P.M.	Break—Someone could have games for the younger set, mothers could tend to their

children's needs, adults could chat a bit and look over the displays.

9:15 P.M.—10:15 P.M. Buffet

10:15 P.M.—11:30 P.M. Film

Singing and Offering

11:30 P.M.— ? Closing comments by your pastor

Testimonies

Prayer Requests

PRAY IN THE NEW YEAR

V. *Menu*

Check with your missionary—he or she might send you cookbooks, recipes and menus. Or check out your local international restaurant. Keep it kosher!

Have your buffet table laden with as many of these specialties as possible. Many people may turn up their noses at some of the dishes, but encourage them to at least *taste*. Small samplings of each dish may open up a whole new world for their tastebuds. They shouldn't be snobs. This could be an exciting new adventure for each family!

You may want to include:

MATZO MEAL DUMPLINGS (Used on Passover)

1 cup Matzo Meal
½ cup water or soup
1 teaspoon salt
1 teaspoon ground ginger
2 eggs, well beaten
4 tablespoons oil

Mix all ingredients together and refrigerate. It is essential that the batter is made at least four hours before cooking, to absorb all the moisture.
Roll balls out of the batter with wet hands. Drop the dumplings into boiling chicken soup, a few at a time, about 30 minutes before serving.
SHALOM!

PROGRAM #2

Valentine Breakfast

This particular program is geared for an all-church emphasis. Many times when we gear February activities to "sweethearts," it eliminates our fast growing number of singles (young and old). So let's concentrate on the "heart" and "love."

Preparations:

1. One month before the set date
   — have an attractive poster on the bulletin board
   — announce the breakfast weekly from the pulpit
   — determine who the cooks will be
   — assign an overall coordinator

2. Two weeks before the set date
   — put a sign-up list on the bulletin board
   (break down into adults—by name)
   (break down into teens—by name)
   (break down into children—by name)
   You will want an exact number.

3. One week before the set date
   — fold all Valentine napkins
   — fill vases with silk flowers
   — make place markers

4. One day before the set date
   — set the tables/make favors
   — decorate the Fellowship Hall
   — cooks do the shopping
   — precook all bacon and sausage

5. Two hours before the set time
   — put last minute items on tables
   — start coffee
   — prepare pancake batter
   — start warming meat in oven

6. Half hour before set time
   — greeter waiting at door
   — parking attendant in place
   — photographer ready for action
   — waiters lined up for serving

8:00 A.M.   — PRAY AND EAT

Approximately 100 people will require the following:

   2 packages of Styrofoam cups (100)
   2 packages of red Solo cups (100) for milk and juice
   5 packages of Valentine napkins (20's)
   2 packages of heavy plastic plates (50's)

   10 tables—tablecloths—centerpieces—tableware

On Tables: syrup   plates
             butter   tableware
             milk   napkins
             sugar   favors
             juice   place markers

Coffee Table: coffee pot
                Styrofoam cups
                trays for men to serve coffee
                extra pouring pitchers

Needed for Valentine Breakfast Menu:

Pancakes	12 pounds of mix
Sausage	15 pounds
Bacon	13 pounds
Coffee	1 pound
Milk	5 gallons
Juice	4 gallons
Eggs	4 dozen (for pancakes)
Butter	3 pounds

| Syrup | 1 gallon |
| Oil | 1 quart (for 4 griddles) |

Placemarkers:
White construction paper cut 4″ x 3″
Red self-sticking hearts
Small Bible stickers

Favors: 100 pink nut cups
3 yards red net
1 roll red ribbon
1 roll white ribbon
2 packages jelly hearts
2 boxes of Waffle O's cereal

Program: Invite a missionary especially talented in reaching the younger set. Possibly he could have a puppet program or use a dummy to present a gospel message.

Following the breakfast, program and cleanup . . . everyone packs up and heads for the nearest snow-covered slope for sledding and tobogganing.

PROGRAM #3

Nursery "plus" Shower

Why a Nursery "plus" Shower? Very simply to pacify those who feel that their favorite ministry is being neglected! So, we settle for a combo deal!

This is an excellent way to furnish the Nursery and Kitchen (for example) of your church, or use it to help a mission church.

In all fairness, this type of combination shower may be more practical for smaller churches where the needs would not be so numerous.

Decide on your "combo"—Nursery plus Kitchen, Nursery plus Toddler, etc.

* * *

Keep the refreshments light, as you will want the ladies to concentrate on purchasing the gift items.

Suggestions: 1. Salad Bowl Buffet—all fruit salads, crackers and cheeses
2. Huge Chef's Salad—hard rolls
3. Dessert Smorgasbord—bring recipes

Choose a seasonal color combination for table center-piece and napkins. Serve a refreshing beverage.

* * *

Include a few games, and ask several ladies to prepare a short testimony. This is an informal gathering. You may find that it will run later than expected—the ladies usually relax and visit.

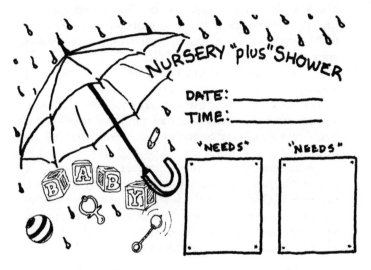

NURSERY "plus" SHOWER

DATE: _____

TIME: _____

"NEEDS"

"NEEDS"

Check (✓) items You are bringing. Luke 18:16

PROGRAM #4

The Preconference Banquet

This time of fellowship will usually climax four weeks of preconference cottage prayer meetings. (If you do not bathe your annual missionary conference in much prayer, you have already missed out on the most vital part of your conference preparations.) The preconference banquet may also be used as the kick-off banquet for your conference. This is a good time for your ·missionaries to each give their personal testimonies, or have a special speaker to challenge the church family and to encourage the conference missionaries.

The annual missionary conference should have top priority among your church programs. More is accomplished for Christ during a missionary conference than during any other special meetings a church will have—salvation—dedication—concentration. . . . Give your *all* for these special meetings.

Make your preconference banquet very special! Follow all the guidelines laid out at the beginning of this section of PROGRAMS. Add a few frills and extras, such as ordering corsages for all the lady missionaries and your pastor's wife! Be extra cooperative with everybody. You'll be surprised how the Lord will bless a willing heart!

Some Pointers:

1. Determine well in advance what the cost of this banquet will be. *Do not* "rob" your missionaries! Banquet expenses should be taken care of long before a missionary arrives in town.

2. If this banquet is for adults only—then have it for adults! If your missions committee desires to have this as a family affair, then plan accordingly.

If the banquet is to include or exclude outside guests, make this very clear to the people of the church.

3. *Do not* use your banquet for a money-making scheme. (This statement may crush some of you.) The current trend is to have a "whoopie-ding" banquet, stuff the guests, hand them a pledge card—then put arsenic in their dessert if the

big figures aren't filled in.

Faith-promises are done in an orderly fashion, by God's people, in an atmosphere of holiness and dedication between God and man. Man's money-making schemes have done more to turn people away from missions than we will ever know.

SAMPLE

AROUND the WORLD with the ADULTS of _____ CHURCH

TIME: 5:30 P.M.
PLACE: FELLOWSHIP ROOM
DATE: APRIL _____ , _____

* * * * * * * * * * * * *

International Smorgasbord

NEW ENGLAND CLAM CHOWDER   CHINESE TEA
SYRIAN SALAD   COFFEE (Hot or Iced)
FRENCH BREAD   ICE TEA (Lemon)
DIXIE CORN BREAD

IRISH STEW
CHICKEN PIE
BEEF STROGANOF
SAUERKRAUT & PORK
MOUSE (Kale & Pork)
LASAGNA
SWEET & SOUR CHICKEN
RUSSIAN POTATOES
BRUSSEL SPROUTS
NORTH AMERICAN "ASKUTASQUASH"

SWEDISH COFFEE CAKE
ENGLISH TEA CAKES
GERMAN CHOCOLATE CAKE
OLD KENTUCKY NUT CAKE

Any Questions? Phone _____

You may check the foods you will be bringing on the bulletin board poster. Thank you!

(Optional) . . . To make the evening festive, you may wear a costume to fit the occasion, featuring any land you desire.

PROGRAM #5

Mother-Daughter Banquet

The entire layout of this banquet is done using the color *pink*—returning to a very feminine flair. The preparations for this program are time consuming, so, please draw up your initial committees and duties at least two months in advance.

I. *Theme: A Living Sacrifice*—Romans 12:1 and 2

Make attractive posters for bulletin boards throughout the church. Be sure to include all essential information which will also be shown on the personal invitations given out.

"A LIVING SACRIFICE"

Friday - May 9, 19__
6:30 p.m.
Special Banquet
Special Guest
Special Surprises
    Please Come!

For all Daughters (Five and up)
& Mothers   Romans 12:1+2

II. *Speaker*

Pray about a speaker—one who is adept at reaching the hearts of this large age span. Your speaker should have some "life," especially if you expect a large group of guests. After a banquet there are those who almost immediately slump into dreamland (old and young alike).

Contact your speaker *early* in the year—be sure to let her know the theme, date, hour, location of church (send a map), the proper attire (long or short dress), and the length of time she may speak. Request a publicity photo, check on food allergies, and invite her to stay over for the night.

After the speaker has accepted your invitation, be sure to send a copy of the program and final confirmation a few weeks before the date (this also serves as a reminder—just in case the speaker has slipped up on her scheduling).

III. *Invitation*

Pass out invitations *three weeks* before the banquet. Be firm regarding reservations. Stick to your cut-off date! Eventually, with your pastor's support, people will realize that you really mean business!

INVITATION COVER

"A LIVING SACRIFICE"

Use 8½ x 5½ PINK mimeo paper.
Fold.
Use fabric lightly glued on to "clothe" the figure on the cover.

INSIDE—

You're invited to _____
                            (name of church)

Address _____

                    *   *   *   *

Mother—Daughter Banquet
Friday, May 9, 19 _____
6:30 P.M.

Special Theme: "A LIVING SACRIFICE"
                        Romans 12:1 and 2
Special Speaker: (Name)
                        A love offering will be taken.
Special Dinner: Served by the men of the
                        church
                        COST: $2.50

Special Requests: Reservations **must** be given to
_____ , (phone) or _____ (phone) no later than
May 2.
(Daughters must be age 5 or older.)

                                    Thank You

                    Sponsored by
            The Ladies' Missionary Fellowship

IV. *Decorations*

1. **Picnic Baskets** . . . . with three shades of pink gera-
niums (live and potted) artisti-
cally placed throughout the
church. These may later be
used in the church flower
bed. (They could also be used
for award gifts.)

2. **Small Baskets** . . . . filled with handmade flowers
of pink dotted swiss or pink
gingham—to be used as table
centerpieces.

3. **Raffia Dolls** . . . . mother and daughter dolls
dressed in pink gingham. Use
as wall decorations . . . later
may be given as gifts to visiting missionaries or used as
awards at the banquet.

4. **Favors** . . . . pink nut cups glued to gold
mini-doilies.

5. **Napkin Holders** . . . . . . use 2″ paper rolls from wax
paper, cover with pink felt,
glue on a pink flower and a
piece of net and place rolled
napkin inside.

6. **Name Tags** . . . . corn-cob faces glued to pink
construction paper with
theme printed on them. Be
sure to put pink gingham sun-
bonnets on the heads.

V. *Menu*

Appetizer—Strawberry Jello Souffle
Relish Dish—Stuffed celery, deviled eggs, cucumber
sticks, pickled beets
Main Course—Turkey breast
Dressing
Mashed potatoes
Corn
Gravy

136

Crescent rolls, butter
Beverage—Pink lemonade, tea, coffee
Dessert—Assorted Tarts*

* These desserts are very attractive. Use mini pastry shells.
 Fillings—pistachio, lemon, coconut cream, chocolate,
  and banana cream pudding
 Toppings—Swirl around the edge with Reddi-whip, put
  a dab in the center and garnish with cherries,
  coconut, chocolate shavings, or slivered
  almonds.

This meal is best served family style, with appetizers and relish dishes already placed on the tables, and men bringing the main course after mothers and daughters are seated.

After the men have cleared away the dirty dishes and food leftovers, they may serve the dessert on large trays, making sure they have a good assortment on each tray.

Ask the men to be sure to check on the beverage needs of the guests.

(To dress up your men, you could ask them to wear white shirts and you could grace their collars with a pink carnation. Or better still, have the ladies make up pink ties for them.)

VI. *Program*

Song . . . Use an easy chorus having the words printed up to make your guests comfortable. It is very embarrassing to see the "church folk" singing up a storm, and the poor visitor wanting to crawl under the table. Be thoughtful about this.

Welcome and Prayer

Dinner

Following the dinner, allow fifteen minutes for the little ones to make that much-needed stop at the restroom before going to the auditorium for the program. Also, use some of your out-going ladies to keep a watchful eye for those who will invariably try to sneak out and to warmly encourage them to stay.

Song	"Living for Jesus"
Poem	Teen Girl
Awards	
Song	"Only To Be"
Message	Missionary
Offering	
Song	"I'll Live for Him"
Closing Prayer	

When using a "full-blown" banquet type of meal—keep your program short!

VII. *Patterns*

PROGRAM COVERS

Dress—pink felt
Sleeve—white sheer fabric
Sleeve cuff—lace
Flowers—from novelty bunches
Hat—black felt
Trim—any kind with white and pink

Pages of program are shaped like the cover—back page is light weight posterboard.

⅜" Corn cobs
Plastic eyes
Red Flair (pen) mouth
Pink gingham sunbonnet
Pink yarn ribbon

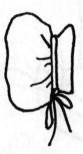

Barb S

"A LIVING TREASURE"

ROMANS 12: 1+2

PROGRAM #6

Father—Son Banquet

A father-son banquet is a wonderful opportunity to express appreciation for the men of the church—the men who have been so supportive of the church mission program. Many of the church fathers have been babysitting, warming up supper, taking the children to McDonalds, and doing the dishes while mother is attending the Ladies' Missionary Fellowship. Men of the church have been known to offer their services to the women by building missionary cupboards, designing light-boxes, bandage rolling stands, and just about anything else to help with the cause of missions. Make this banquet very special for some very special men.

I. *Theme—***"A Chip Off the Old Block"**

> Verse: *And he shall be like a tree planted by the rivers of water, that bringeth forth his fruit in his season; his leaf also shall not wither; and whatsoever he doeth shall prosper (Ps. 1:3).*

II. *Decorations*

1. Have a church artist paint a fully leafed tree on posterboard, with a hatchet and wedge at the base of the tree. Have a place marked on each leaf for the fathers and sons to sign their names. Use this poster for promotion (be sure to have the proper information printed on it).

2. Gather up as many old-fashioned tools for chopping down trees as you can locate—a crossbuck saw, hatchets, a come-along, ropes, axes, wedges, etc. Place these items around the Fellowship Room.

3. Have one large bulletin board in the Fellowship Room covered in pale green paper—have the theme verse cut out of brown letters on the board, along with attractive pictures of trees, men and boys.

4. Use brown streamers down the center of your tables, green napkins, and nut cups filled with small pretzels.

III. *Menu*

CHILLED TOMATO JUICE
ROAST BEEF AND GRAVY
BAKED POTATO AND SOUR CREAM
BUTTERED CORN
TOSSED SALAD
LEMONADE/COFFEE—ROLLS/BUTTER—PICKLES
STRAWBERRY SHORTCAKE

IV. *Invitation* (Include menu if desired)

ALL FATHERS . . . ALL SONS . . .

YOU ARE INVITED TO THE
FATHER-SON BANQUET
JUNE 14, 19 _____ AT 6:30 P.M.
AT .
_____CHURCH

RESERVATIONS (BY JUNE 8)

AGE 12 THRU ADULTS $1.50
UNDER AGE 12 . . . . $1.00
(An offering will be taken also.)

V. *Program*   GET ACQUAINTED TIME—GAMES
MUSICAL PACKAGE—COLLEGE QUARTET
SPEAKER—REPRESENTATIVE FROM MISSIONS
DEPARTMENT OF COLLEGE
FILM—"STRANGERS FROM GALILEE"

A Chip Off the Old Block

PROGRAM #7

Hawaiian Luau

This particular program takes a lot of *work,* but it has been one of the more festive and well-received socials. It offers a good opportunity for people to spend the day working and playing together. Many are involved in the cooking preparations, and the host home usually has facilities for yard games — softball, volleyball, horseshoes and "hammock."

I. *Dress*

Men — wild, flowered shirts (you'd be surprised how many men really enjoy dressing "wild" — even the most reserved of them).

Women — bright flowered muumuus (some like to get together and make their dresses).

Leis — can be bought at your local party novelty shop (unless you have a church friend flying in from the Islands with the real thing).

II. *Decorations*

Lots of pretty color — fresh cut flowers on tables, seashells, starfish, fishing nets can be arranged on the buffet table. Japanese lanterns hanging in the trees.

III. *Menu*

ROAST PIG*	RICE
CHICKEN TERIYAKI	WATER CHESTNUTS/
FISH ON THE GRILL	CHICKEN LIVERS
STEAMED CLAMS (if	SAUTEED MUSHROOMS
readily available)	STUFFED TOMATOES
	ROASTED CORN ON
	COB

144

FRESH FRUIT BASKET
Basket: Halve and scoop out a watermelon
Use all *fresh* fruits:

watermelon chunks	BEACH BOY PUNCH
pineapple strips	1 quart cranberry juice
strawberries	1 pint orange juice
melon balls	juice of 2 lemons
blueberries	2 quarts ginger ale
light syrup	

This is a very rich meal, so use the fruit basket for dessert.

NIBBLER: FRESH COCONUT CHIPS

*Roast Pig — men need to prepare a good size pit — fill it with charcoal — build a support for a large "spit" — and prepare to spend *all day* taking turns at the handle.

Note: Do not tie the pig shut — leave the legs spread open to hasten the cooking process. Also, have some munchin' food out by the pit for the men. (The cooked tail is considered a delicacy by some people.)

IV. *Program*

Since this is such a relaxed social, there may be many unsaved visitors watching and listening! Keep your testimony sweet and pure (even if you strike out during the softball game!) — and please make the visitors feel welcome!

Be sure to have a guest speaker who can adapt to any given situation — a missionary who is good at mingling with the people (not all can do this, you know).

After cooking, playing games and eating — sit back for a "chorus" sing and a *short,* meaningful devotional by the missionary. Invite everyone to come to church the next morning to hear more from your missionary.

V. *Tips*

Have a camera bug on hand for some very interesting candid shorts. There will be plenty!

As a church member, don't play visitor at this affair — the hostess may end up a basket-case from exhaustion. Some of the younger women could be "gofers" and ease the leg work. Don't hestitate to snoop for extra ice cubs when needed, serve up seconds on punch, or wipe up a spill!

To pretty-up your punch — make an ice ring ahead of time, place washed plastic flowers in the ring (tape across top of ring or flowers will float) and freeze.

Such a fun, fun day . . . . enjoy it!   ALOHA

PROGRAM #8

Teen Picnic

Our homes need to be opened to the teens of the church, even the homes where there are no children. Many times older couples have a real burden for the youth and can use their experiences in life to be a blessing to some young person. In a given number of teens, you can be sure to find some unsaved and some in need of guidance.

Invite a missionary to share his or her testimony and give a challenge from God's Word. This should be in an informal atmosphere, possibly sitting out on the grass around the fire, or sitting cross-legged on your living room floor.

Meet at an hour when you can get in several games of volleyball or softball. Plan your picnic for the sunset hour. Then settle down for a chorus sing followed by the missionary speaker. Be sure to close out your evening with an invitation; hearts will be softened and opened by the warm time of fellowship.

Picnic

Keep it simple . . . let teens prepare and cook the foods.

Guys: Set up the fires, cook the meat, plan games, lead singing.

Gals: Make the salads, punch, chili sauce, dips.

MENU

TOSSED SALAD
CORN ON COB
HOT DOGS WITH CHILI SAUCE
HAMBURGERS
CHIPS 'n DIPS
PUNCH
S'MORS FOR DESSERT

PROGRAM #9

Fall Roundup

After a very busy summer of gardening, vacationing, D.V.B.S., canning, children — it takes an extra-special social to zero in on the important church programs. To accomplish this feat in the area of missions, it is advisable to organize a Fall Roundup among several area churches (ones that share your separatist stand). It could also be called an Area-Wide Missionary Rally.

A Fall Roundup brings together groups of women willing to exchange ideas on programs and projects in order to provoke some enthusiasm for the work. This has been a very successful meeting in my experience. Women have left with renewed vision, new avenues of work to explore, and a special warmth that radiates from the fellowship of such a meeting.

It usually takes one person to instigate such a rally. She puts the bug in a few ears, an organizational meeting takes place, plans are drawn up, invitations are made, and you're on your way!

I. *Theme*

"SERVE THE LORD WITH GLADNESS"

Psalm 100

II. *Decorations*

1. Allow the host church to determine the decorations suitable for the occasion. Some churches desire to follow through with seasonal colors and flowers, while others prefer to use materials more suited to the theme.

2. Should you wish to use place mats, napkins or novelties associated with missions, these may be purchased from

Wright Studios
5638 East Washington Street
Indianapolis, Indiana 46219

A catalogue listing will be sent upon request.

III. *Program*

1. Because of the nature of this meeting, plan to use women from the different churches represented beforehand and during this program.

You will need individuals for invitations, ushers, greeters, name tags, projects coordinator and food chairman.

2. Each church should bring samples of their work to be put out on display. One church could be responsible for overseeing this display.

3. **A sample program:**

9:45 A.M. Ladies arrive (register & name tags)
10:00 A.M. Welcome
        Prayer
        Recognition of churches
        Song
        Workshop Time:*

P = PRINCIPLE . . .
   = PURPOSE . . .
   = PROJECTS . . .
   = PROGRAM . . .

        Musical Special
11:30 A.M. Lunch
        Look over projects

1:00 P.M. Prayer
        Skit**
        Message (Visiting missionary on the theme)
        Closing

* These topics should be divided among four women, each having fifteen minutes to share her thoughts relating the topics to the Ladies' Missionary Fellowship.

** Skits are available from

Baptist Mid-Missions
4205 Chester Ave.
Cleveland, Ohio 44103

4. Two *goals* to consider are training and encouragement. New Christians need to be challenged and taught. Older Christians need to be challenged and encouraged.

IV. *Menu*

Since the women will be bringing in foods, keep it fairly simple. The host church should provide all the paper goods and beverages.

Buffet: Dress it up by using your best serving trays.

> DEVILED EGGS
> FANCY SWEET PICKLES
> CHEESES
> CRACKERS — USE VARIETY
> SALADS: TUNA
>   SALMON
>   CHICKEN
>   MACARONI
>   POTATO
>   JELLO (WITH VEGETABLES)
> MINI CHEESECAKES
> COFFEE — TEA — PUNCH
> NUTS — MINTS

V. *Suggestion*

Your Ladies' Missionary Fellowship will be "on fire" when the day is over. Don't let the fire go out! Instead, start making plans for this year's mission program and even set up another rally for next year.

PROGRAM #10

Preconference Tupperware Shower

The object of this program is to fill your missionary cupboard with all sizes and shapes of Tupperware. It must be emphasized to all concerned that this is *not* a money-making endeavor — it does not betray your church constitution regarding church monies! It simply involves purchasing desired gifts for missionaries. Any accumulated credits usually are turned in for additional pieces of Tupperware, or they go toward the purchase of the bonus gift item.

Once again, keep the refreshments on the light side so as not to detract from the purchasing of gift items.

Do not neglect to have a missionary speaker, a mission slide presentation, or a mission devotional by one of the ladies.

Make an effort to locate a *Christian* Tupperware dealer — otherwise, you may find yourself apologizing for some unsavory language from a worldly woman. This would be inappropriate and offensive.

I. *Favors*

Use seasonal colors —

You may ask, "Why favors?" Arranged attractively on your buffet table, they serve as edible decorations. They also eliminate the need for a candy-nut tray. They're pretty and taste good!

II. *Menu*

A "veggie" platter with dips — carrot sticks, celery sticks, broccoli spears, cauliflower buds, and scallions
Open-faced sandwiches — Ham & Swiss on Party Rye
Rosettes, Pecan Tassies (flour and cream cheese dough filled with brown sugar and pecan mixture), and Apricot-filled Thumbprint Cookies
Constant Comment Orange or Spice Tea
Lemonade (Season will determine the beverage)

SAMPLE

PROGRAM #11

Harvest Banquet

This seasonal program has always been a sheer delight to organize. Good spirits and cooperation have always been received from all concerned persons — from workers to guests! Maybe it is because everyone has just finished a productive summer of gardening and canning and, realizing that winter will soon set in, are desirous to share their harvest at a good old-fashioned time of fellowship. Perhaps it is the lull before the hustle and bustle of the months to follow. Whatever the reason, this has always rated the highest attendance and greatest blessing among the people.

I. *Theme — The Harvest*
1. The Scripture verses are endless for this theme. Many verses relate to "harvest" or "thanksgiving"!

. . . The harvest truly is great, but the labourers are
few: pray ye therefore the Lord of the harvest, that
he would send forth labourers into his harvest (Luke
10:2).

. . . Be thankful unto him, and bless his name. For
the Lord is good . . . (Ps. 100:4 and 5).

1. Decide exactly what you desire to accomplish from this banquet, whether it is to challenge your people in the area of thankfulness, giving or working for missions, sharing, dedication, soul winning, compassion, etc. All of these could be incorporated into one thrust if handled in the right way — **missions!**

2. After locating your theme verse, have someone make a very special banner with the verse in bold lettering. Place this banner where people will see it on a regular basis for several weeks before the banquet.

Many churches use the auditorium walls for promotional reasons. If the lettering is neat and in good taste, fine; but, some people do not appreciate defacing the sanctuary for any reason — especially if it is behind the pastor and distracts the people. Use discretion in this matter. If it causes an offense to some, use this type of promotion sparingly. After all, there are hallways and bulletin boards available in most churches.

3. Over the years it has been beneficial to invite veteran missionaries as guest speakers because they have so much to share about spiritual harvesting! Oh, the joy of listening to them share their lives with people and to weep while observing true compassion in action.

II. *Decorations*

1. Seek out someone who has creative ability and can lead in this area. Keep your eyes open as you visit church folks. If a person is "crafty," it shows in the home!

2. Go natural! In the fall there are many beautiful

ways to decorate from your own yard or nearby woods.

> CHRYSANTHEMUMS (all shades of red, gold,
>   bronze)
> MARIGOLDS (they last right up to frost)
> FIREBUSHES
> WHEATS
> AUTUMN LEAVES
> BERRY BUSHES
> CORN STALKS
> GOURDS
> PUMPKINS
> APPLES
> GRAPES
> NUTS

3. Check out the corners of your cellars or basements for antique baskets, barrels, grinders, kettles, jars, crocks, and scales to hold the fall gatherings. These can be beautifully displayed.

4. Take advantage of this beautiful season of the year. Fall can be an artist's delight!

III. *Program*

1. Because of the large number of guests, it would be well to use an "ice-breaker" (sample on next page).

2. Use name tags — an autumn leaf cut out of gold or orange construction paper — easy and inexpensive. Also, encourage church members to mingle; don't allow "cliques" to sit together.

3. A good order might be:
> "Ice-breaker"
> Singing (in auditorium)
> Welcome (by pastor)
> Directions (as to seating in the Fellowship
>   Room and serving of the food)
> Prayer
> Eat and Fellowship (allow time for this to be
>   a relaxed affair — don't rush)*
> Guest speaker (in auditorium)

154

Warm farewells to visitors

*Any prizes or awards should be given at this time.

SAMPLE

"ICE-BREAKER"

SENSE 'N NONSENSE . . .

"WHO'S WHO AT _____ BAPTIST CHURCH"

1. *Initials* of someone born in New England.
2. A *man* with a nick-name ending in a vowel.
3. A woman with brown hair and brown eyes — NOT a mother.
4. Someone who has been on *foreign* soil within the past two years.
5. Someone who has *never* been in an airplane.
6. Someone who *is* or *has been* a public school teacher.
7. SILENT NIGHT is *one!*
8. A father of *three* or *more* children.
9. Who never *loses?*
10. Someone who *does not* like seafood.
11. What do you receive *each month* in the mail?
12. Who is always *fretting?*
13. Someone born *outside* of North America.
14. The *early* morning hours?
15. Nick-name is a large marble!
16. *Initials* of a person who likes to hunt.

* * * * * * * * * * * * *

Use the turkey pattern on the following page. Cut the turkeys out of orange construction paper and give one to each guest along with a copy of the above list. The person who completes the list first is the winner. Have a small token gift.

155

LOCATE THE PERSONS WHO FIT THE "SENSE 'N NON-
SENSE" LIST . . . HAVE *THEM* FILL IN THEIR NAMES ON
THE TURKEY FEATHERS . . . *DO NOT* REPEAT NAMES.

IV. Menu

Thanksgiving started in New England, so nothing can top the basic New England menu! It is yummy from beginning to end! This is part of our national heritage . . . try it, and you will like it!

Appetizer (or "fellowship nibblers" before the meal)

DISHES OF THREE VARIETIES OF GRAPES, WASHED AND NICELY ARRANGED

NUTS — IN THE SHELL (PROVIDE NUTCRACKERS)
CHILLED CIDER

Main Course

ROAST TURKEY	CORN
STUFFING	CREAMED ONIONS
GRAVY	CRANBERRY SAUCE
SQUASH	HOMEMADE BREADS

Dessert

HOMEMADE PIES — APPLE, MINCEMEAT, PUMPKIN

Beverage

CIDER — GINGER ALE — TEA — COFFEE

Extra

NUT CUPS — CANDY CORN

Now, can you imagine the "culture shock" of a young missionary wife on her first term in Africa — with a Thanksgiving meal carrying no resemblance to the above meal? She went deep down into her barrels to locate a can of creamed corn for her reminder of the family Thanksgivings in America. The grace that God gave this woman as she served Him the many years in Africa! You should see the peace and joy in her blue eyes now as her two sons and their families are serving the Lord on the mission field.

"The Lord is good and greatly to be praised"

PROGRAM #12

Christmas Tea

Although this is called a "tea," it is more like a dressed-up *buffet*. It is an opportunity to bring out all your special dishes, polish your silver and really put on the dog. This is also a time to include your teen girls — use this as part of their training. Encourage everyone to dress up for this affair.

I. *Theme*

Then spake Jesus again unto them, saying, I am the light of the world: he that followeth me shall not walk in darkness, but shall have the light of life (John 8:12).

II. *Decorations*

1. **Place Cards** . . . Prepare the cards, glue a toothpick on back, stick into either a large marshmellow or large red gumdrop at each plate. Be sure to have a "friendly" hostess seated at each table.

2. **Centerpieces** . . . Two are shown here — both very simple but pretty.

III. *Special*

Craft Exchange — "Yankee Swap"

Each lady and girl makes a craft gift. Use a "number grab" to receive your gift. If another person has a gift you would like, you have two chances to exchange. After the second round, you keep the gift in your possession.

IV. *Program*

SPECIAL MUSIC .... Musical package by teen girls
FIELD REPORT .... Visiting missionary
DEVOTIONS .... Visiting missionary
FILM .... No more than 30 minutes
CHRISTMAS MEDITATIONS .... Pastor's wife
CLOSING CHRISTMAS SONG AND PRAYER

* * * * * * * * * * * *

Begin your program at 6:30 sharp! Keep it moving! The Christmas buffet will be served immediately following the program.

After the buffet has been eaten, relax for an informal time of fellowship and the craft exchange. At this time you may want to surprise your pastor's wife with Christmas baked goods — each person brings a Christmas specialty all wrapped along with the recipe to help your pastor's wife with the holiday entertaining.

V. *Menu*

TURKEY A LA KING   (Served in pastry shells)

159

*Seafood Delight
(Optional — since ingredients may not be readily available everywhere!)

CRANBERRY JELLO SALAD
MUSHROOMS AND PEAS
CRISPY BUTTERED ROLLS
*CHRISTMAS PUNCH
*TEA

*Have teen girls attend the beverage table.

GOODIE TRAY — Fudge, pastries, mini-fruitcakes

*Seafood Delight
(Serves 16 — 20)

1 lb. Filet of Haddock	Using a large chicken fryer and 3 cups
2 lb. Fresh Scallops	lightly salted boiling water — "poach"
1 lb. Shrimp (Jumbo)	fish gently until barely cooked (separ-
1 lb. Lobster Meat	ately). Set aside in large deep bowl and cover to keep moist.

Strain cooking stock into a heavy 5-quart pot.

Add: ⅛ cup finely minced onion, ¼ cup finely minced green pepper, ½ tsp. Lawry's Salt, ½ tsp. Worcestershire, ½ tsp. Paprika

Simmer 5 minutes — add ½ cup *butter* — when melted, add 1 pint light cream. When just at the scalding point add a smooth running paste of ¾ cup flour and cold milk. Cook til smooth and *thick*. Add 1 cup sliced stuffed olives. Gently mix fish to distribute varieties. Then pour hot sauce over fish and allow to settle one hour. Bake in two 2-quart casserole dishes. Top with fine bread crumbs. Decorate with claws and shrimp. Bake at 325 degrees until golden and bubbly, about ½ hour.

CLOSING COMMENTS

LOOKING BACK . . .

Sitting here in my home, looking out at the beautiful New Hampshire scenery, reflecting upon the past years of my life, the question hits me, "What have *I* done for Jesus?" People still doubt, people still search, people still need to be saved.

"Also I heard the voice of the Lord, saying, Whom shall I send, and who will go for us? then said I, Here am I; send me" (Isa. 6:8).

No, my steps have not taken me onto any foreign soil. No, my name is not on the roster of any mission board. We can all look back and say, "I should have done this or that," but we forget that God knows all things from the beginning to the end. How I praise His glorious name for affording me the privilege of working with so many of His faithful servants. It is with a thankful heart that I acknowledge the full support, encouragement and generosity of my husband in opening our home to well over one hundred missionaries. Also, a real note of appreciation to our five children for surrendering their bedrooms and helping in so many ways with the preparations for entertaining.

It is with warm memories that we can laugh and muse over the many occasions when a missionary was part of our household. Some would not eat pork, some did not drink tea or coffee, some guzzled tonic (pop or soda); there were the flea market hoppers, the antique collectors, the ice cream lovers, the special diets, the "night" people, the "day" people, the shoppers, the talkers, the readers, the late arrivers, the tired ones, the hyper ones — each one has a special place in our hearts.

Our children have their own personal memories. Like the "missionary kids" who "cooked" all the fish in our daughter's aquarium when they turned up the water heater. Diane took it very well! There was the "special" cake baked by Lorraine for the president of the mission board — she forgot to include one ingredient, and it came out a heavy, soggy lump. The gentlemen was a real gentlemen — he ate it! Our daughter, Joyce, was spellbound by a very special missionary from Timbuktu — she hung on his every word. She received her one and only A+ in geography by giving a superb report on that country. Ruth (Ruthie or Rufus) automatically knew it was the "floor or couch" if a missionary was coming. Of course this gave way to a good excuse to soak up all the late evening conversations which she thoroughly enjoyed. Ah, yes, and Stuart — he was the luggage toter! Stu was also the first of our children to realize that missionaries are *people*. He always enjoyed the chatter and the debates around the kitchen table (along with the food). When Stu would check the refrigerator and see extra goodies — he knew — the missionaries were coming!

How has this affected our lives? Diane, now a wife and mother of two sons, is slowly "picking up the mantle." She has a warm, open heart toward missions — corresponding with some on the mission field, buying special gifts and sewing for others, praying and burdened for particular ones. Stuart is also married with one son, and he still finds joy and encouragement in the presence of missionaries. His home is open to any who are in his area, and he still enjoys assisting in whatever way possible. The other three girls are not married, but on different occasions we talk about things that impressed them personally. Ruth is away at Baptist Bible College — hmmm, maybe?

Looking Ahead . . .

Bill and I have gone back to "square one" now. The children are grown and the table is set for two once again. The rocking chair and clubs are not for us! A new era is unfolding before us, one with unlimited hours of service for our Lord. My husband is back in school preparing for what God would have him to do. His heart is burdened for soul winning and visitation. Missions — hometown U.S.A.! As for me, my heart's desire is to continue in missions until that day when Jesus comes. I pray that God will use this book to stir up the hearts of those who have "relaxed" in their mission endeavors. That He would redirect where some churches are using mission funds to promote Christian schools and bus ministries, a distinct hindrance to the mission program of the local church. Hundreds of missionaries are waiting for financial and prayer support. How long shall we keep them waiting?

In Conclusion . . .

Allow me to share a letter from a missionary friend in Brazil. I've asked her to comment on her feelings about the benefits of having a missionary cupboard.

"My, what pretty dishes these are! Where did you get them from?" one of my guests asked . . .

"From a missionary cupboard in New Jersey," was my reply . . .

"Oh, what gorgeous sheets and pillow cases and they match your bed so well," remarked another missionary friend as she shared my joy in receiving my barrels . . .

"Yes, aren't they nice? . . . and I didn't even have to shell out money for them. I got them from a missionary cupboard in New England," again was my reply . . .

"Oh, thank you for those sleeveless shirts for the baby! I've looked all over this town for them and they just don't exist," was the excited cry of a national believer who had just given birth to a baby boy. These also were given by another church in New England.

When I have a big number of people for dinner, I am reminded of yet another church in New Jersey that gave me my 24-piece setting of melmac and silverware.

These were direct quotes and definite items received that brought much joy to the receiver, and yet many wonder if missionary cupboards and showers are worth it.

My answer is a definite, resounding "YES" for the following reasons:

They save much:

time — which missionaries have very little of

energy — not having to shop from store to store

money — enough of which is never available for things which may seem a luxury to some, but very indispensible for those of us on the field . . .

They are very definite reminders, as they are used, of:

Friends back home who care to supply needed items (other than money)

Love and concern shown by the hours spent making a coverlet, stuffed animals, throw pillow, etc., etc., etc., . . .

Sometimes when Mishes (missionaries) are unpacking, we murmur about "broken backs" bending deep into barrels, about how much more convenient it would be to have the money instead and do the shopping on the field, which is also very useful and practical. But we need to balance this with very definite items to lace us with people back home, remembering the occasions where we received this, that and another item, and remembering without fail the person who gave such-and-such an item, which gives us that link so very vital to our emotional well-being, connecting us to "home base" . . .

Aggie